CCTE Monographs and Special Publications

General Editor:
Ian Pringle

Writing Narrative — and Beyond

Writing Narrative
— and Beyond

by

John Dixon and Leslie Stratta

 THE CANADIAN COUNCIL OF TEACHERS OF ENGLISH

First published 1986 by
The Canadian Council of Teachers of English

ISBN 0-920472-07-9

The publication of this book was supported in part by grants
from the Pandora Trust.

Printed in Canada

ACKNOWLEDGEMENTS

Our investigation of achievements in writing began in 1979 with a grant from the Schools Council; it still continues, with the support of the Southern Regional Examining Board. We should like to thank Leslie Kant and Lea Orr of the Council, and Henry Macintosh and Robert Osborne of the Board for the encouragement they have consistently given us throughout this period.

From its early days our investigation was based on seminars, first with chief examiners of the CEE boards, next with those of the CGE/CSE boards, and more recently with a joint group of teacher-examiners from the Southern Regional Examination Board. We recall with pleasure the excitement of the discoveries we jointly made. At that early period, too, one individual made a particularly important contribution: Dr Irene Farmer of Bretton Hall College, Wakefield, Yorkshire.

For the pieces of writing discussed here we are indebted to: JMB/TWYLREB and their first exemplar folders of course work; the CEE examiners and the course work material they selected for our seminars; and our friends and colleagues, Margaret Atkin, Pauline Cowan-Monaghan, Sue Crump, John Foggin, Brian Hirst, Eric King, Marsha Looysen, Joan Markham, Bernard Newsom, Paul Norgate and their students. People like these have helped to reveal what a whole range of our students are capable of producing.

For permission to reproduce copyright material, we should like to thank the Southern Regional Examining Board, Macmillan Education (U.K.), the English Centre of the Inner London Education Authority, and the Afro-Caribbean Education Resource Centre, Wyvil Street, London SW8.

Our special thanks are due to Ian Pringle for encouraging us to write this book and to CCTE for undertaking publication.

Finally, this book is undoubtedly in part a reponse to the stimulus and enthusiasm of some hundreds of teachers with whom we have discussed students' achievements in writing — in the U.K., in Canada (especially Winnipeg), in the U.S.A., in Australia (especially Bathurst and Melbourne) and in New Zealand. We have tried to harvest here a few of the many things they taught us.

CONTENTS

Page

Acknowledgements .... (v)

Introduction .... (ix)

CHAPTER 1 : Stories About Ourselves: a human propensity 1

Achievements in an elementary story 2

A more confident writer 5

Some signs of development 6

Suggestions for a model of development 8

Diagnosing constraints on story construction 12

CHAPTER 2 : A Wider Circle of Social Experience 15

An elementary narrative report 16

Diagnosing new demands on the writer 17

Moving into a more complex account 18

Some further demands on the writer 20

Coming to terms with social pressures 21

When does narrative particularise, when does it typify? 24

CHAPTER 3 : Imaginary Stories: Why invent fictions? 27

Why write imaginary stories? 28

Achievements in an elementary story 28

A more confident writer 30

Signs of development? 31

Penetrating even further into an individual consciousness 33

Maturer signs of development 36

Perspective and the choice of narrator 37

Moving into wider social and political experience 38

How can teachers help? 44

What counts as experience? 44

Significant context of people, setting or era 45

How to deal with time 46

Perspective and choice of narrator 46

CHAPTER 4 : Moving Beyond Narrative 49

A natural bridge beyond narrative: Considering people in
general terms 50

A more mature writer : Signs of further achievement .. 52

Study of people in a social world 55

Implications for teaching 57

New structures of discourse emerging 59

CHAPTER 5 : A Further Natural Bridge Beyond Narrative 61
            A Discussing and arguing about behaviour 61
                Discussion that draws on wider (public) knowledge ... 64
                Discussing behaviour more impersonally 66
                Implications for teaching 69
                Further structures of discourse 70

CHAPTER 6 : Looking Further Afield — New Roles 73
                Offering advice: an elementary example 73
                Implications for teaching 76
                Taking an investigation deeper 76
                Implications for teaching 79
                Responding to social pressure 79
                Implications for teaching 80
                Making a cultural statement 81
                Further structures of discourse 83

            Envoi 84

            References 87

INTRODUCTION

This book sets out to break new ground. First, it is about students' achievements. You can treat it, if you wish, as an anthology that demonstrates what students aged 12-18 (and across the ability range) are capable of producing. This in itself is a sort of manifesto, proclaiming what English can offer in a humane education.

Second, it tries to read and explore students' writing in new ways. We read each piece positively, discovering an array of features that contribute to its achievement — offering detailed evidence of insight, understanding and thought. Even the most elementary writing reveals features that attract and delight a sympathetic reader. So we are attempting to educate ourselves and our colleagues as intelligent readers of English compositions in all their variety.

Third, turning to the teaching of writing, we ask which of these features represent points of development. How can teachers read these achievements as signs of progress from more elementary to more complex human understanding? The answers we offer are tentative here. Nevertheless, they cumulatively suggest new perspectives on students' work, and deeper understanding of the challenges students face as they attempt more and more complex ways of shaping experience into words.

Thus, fourth, we briefly discuss strategies for the teacher, to promote students' engagement and progress. Equally, we analyse features in the discourse (whether narrative or beyond) which make new demands on the writer yet offer new opportunities, if they can be mastered with appropriate encouragement and help.

Finally, in one sense, this book is a statement about the English curriculum and *some* of its underlying aims. Not all of them, we hasten to add. This is just one selection from the rich harvest of English teaching over the last 10-20 years. We expect to see many more which will extend our own understanding of what can be gained from writing that springs from personal and social experience — the theme of this book.

Equally, there is at least one further book to be written on writing that is aroused by the reading and presenting of literature and by studies in the media — domains we are actively investigating with colleagues.

CHAPTER 1

Stories about ourselves

A human propensity

Listen in the staffroom. Listen in the bar. Listen to children as they meet again at school on Monday mornings. Listen to ourselves as we get home from a day at work that's been specially memorable. Listen to people meeting in the street. If you don't overhear stories on many of these occasions, we'd be very surprised! And surely some — if not most — will be about the speakers and people they know.

Some will be about a (surprising, galling, hilarious, overwhelming . . .) chain of events. But look out for the moments when the speakers (including yourself) take on a role, break into dramatised dialogue — acting out the facial expression, the gesture, the stance . . . . See them pause, and perhaps look out into space, as they comment reflectively on someone's actions or motives. Notice the shifts of pace, the dramatic pauses, the rising pitch, a sudden lowering of the voice. If it's a story that involves them deeply, see how the past physically grasps them as they relive it.

Then observe the listeners, especially when the speakers are telling stories in which they themselves are involved. The story-tellers have something to share or enforce: what signs are the listeners offering back? — of interest, involvement, empathy, understanding . . . of amusement, shock, irritation, pity . . . ? And how do those signs in their turn seem to affect the speaker (including yourself, remember)?

Everyday life presents us with many different reasons — many different kinds of compulsion — for telling stories about ourselves. You have a problem and you want to get if off your chest — to find a sympathetic ear. You might even want help and advice. Alternatively, you want to make a point: a story is a graphic way of stating and showing what you believe. And how about the stories you tell that simply enhance the way your friends view you — or are self-mocking for that matter? Some stories are trivial and gossipy. Some are a central part of the history of the family (or the neighbourhood, or even the whole nation). Others extend and revise your view of your own history. Sometimes the listener is going to face the same kind of experience — and wants to know what it's like.

What we have been observing, then, is a human propensity. This is why we have chosen to take personal stories first, in our discussion of writing. Not all schools recognise their value, it is true. Nevertheless, for the last generation or more, many teachers of English have tried to build an established tradition of oral and written personal stories.

We believe that, if we attend to it, this natural propensity has much to teach us about written stories in schools. Probably the first lesson for us is that we must make room for them. There is an enormously wide range: let us begin with those that present close, personal relationships with friends or family.

Achievements in an elementary story

Reading positively
Suppose we started like this. Here is a story written by a 15-16 year-old. Have a glance at it and put down your first impressions.

The Outcast
I have got a friend and his name is les he comes up to his Grans every week and he works at the Back of the Kelvin flats he is 17 years old we go to the Baths every week and one week we went one Girl kept her eyes on les and I knew it But les didnt after a bit i told him about the Girl and he went red all of a sudden and showing off he started throwing me about in the water and Ducking me after everything he did he looked at the girl so I thought that I should go over and ask the Girl if She would go out with him and She Said yes then I went Back over and asked les I had already to him that she Said yes and he Said he didnt know and went Back in the water and Started Showing off again throwing me in the water he was ducking me and he was Still red and he was Blushing then it was time for me and les to go out, he wasnt reraly Bothered about the Girl So we went home.

We wonder how many teachers, partly because of our introductory words, partly because of traditions of "marking" rather than responding, would offer comments something like these:

— no control over full stops (points);
— erratic use of upper case;
— no capital for proper name;
— uses casual forms such as "didn't;"
— limited to simple sentence structures;
— simple, everyday vocabulary — few adjectives, for example;
— rather undeveloped story — even trite?
— too short for a student of this age . . . .

In the U.K. at least we have every reason to believe that this tradition is still widespread. A recent national survey by Her Majesty's Inspectors (1979), commenting on a "negative, censorious and possibly counter-productive" tradition — we like the use of "possibly"! — quoted what appears to be a typical set of comments, in this case in the work of a "very able" 15-16 year-old girl. The total sequence for a term follows:

> Not thought out — Full stops and caps not clearly written — Errors of fact — You write a letter as briefly as possible — Needs more careful thought — Not developed — Padding — You have not thought this out sufficiently — Is this all? — Weak — Not what you were told to do — Keep it clear, concise and simple; spoilt by carelessness; tenses — Keep it clear, concise and simple — Argument poor; repetition — Poorly expressed — Meaningless — Rubbish — Last paragraph muddled — Last paragraph shows thought.

Significantly, we believe, the teacher "*spoke* well of this pupil" (our emphasis): what is betrayed in these comments is the assumption that to "mark" is to ferret out errors.

Suppose we try again. Could we ask you to go back and read that story aloud — with a commitment to bringing out the best in it. Then, imagine that this was the optimum achievement of a struggling writer (as it was). If you read it again closely, with that oral version in mind, what positive elements of story-telling would you say that the writer has begun to grasp?

In the diagram below we reproduce some of the suggestions made by teachers in seminars, where we have looked closely at this story.

The Outcast

I have got a friend and his name is les he comes up to his Grans every week and he works at the Back of the Kelvin flats he is 17 years old we go to the Baths every week and one week we went one Girl kept her eyes on les and I knew it But les didnt after a bit I told him about the Girl and he went red all of a sudden and showing off he started throwing me about in the water and Ducking me after everything he did he looked at the girl so I thought that I should go over and ask the Girl if She would go out with him and She Said yes then I went Back over and asked les I had already to him that she Said yes and he Said he didnt know and went Back in the water and Started Showing off again throwing me in the water he was ducking me and he was Still red and he was Blushing then it was time for me and les to go out, he wasnt reraly Bothered about the Girl So we went home.

bare, economic introduction (Les's name, place of work and — significantly — age)

shrewdness (the narrator perceives more than Les, and begins to shape the action)

irony (Les is shown as physically powerful, but emotionally less poised)

assured control (the narrator is neatly in command of what to do next)

cool observation (Les's confused feelings are represented to us through his reactions)

amused dismissal (?) at the end

"It rings true — just like kids I know." "It's amusing too — this lad enjoys a certain sense of power, compared with his friend." "You can imagine — and possibly read into it — all sorts of nods, winks and glances to his friends, as the story is read aloud in class." These are the sorts of summary comments teachers make as they actively construct the potential meaning of the story. The point is that this is a story many teachers actually enjoyed. And, as we have shown, *given that enjoyment,* they were able to articulate in detail many of the features that produced that pleasure.

What we do next

We have read stories like this by many other 11-16 year-olds; it seems to represent a powerful strand in the way they see life. The prime focus is on external actions, and this writer is learning to observe them quite closely at times. But the significance of the actions in this story — throwing, ducking, blushing — is the powerful, confused feelings that lie behind them. There is a tacit psychological understanding underlying these observations.

This story, then, is a reminder that as teachers we have to be very alert for the moments when surface behaviour signifies unarticulated feelings. And those feelings may be — as here — pretty well universal.

As teachers there are two things we might like to do next. The first is to see that it is read aloud in class, bringing out its positive qualities as powerfully as possible. The second is to make room for a discussion in response to it (and other similar stories, perhaps), hoping not only to savour the experience it offers but to explore that situation — the confusions of feeling, the embarrassment, the inarticulacy. We may not be sure whether a writer at this stage *can* go further than "he wasn't reraly Bothered" but we can imagine a relaxed classroom discussion exploring parallel experiences and potentially resonant moments already touched on, such as:

— the first reactions when you tell Les (or similar friend) about a girl who has her eye on him;
— what might be going through your mind — or Les's — if you'd said you "didn't know;"
— why Les might be "showing off" . . . .

This more explicit kind of speculation may then allow room for us to return and say wryly, "I wonder what Les really felt, when he 'wasn't bothered'?"

We have to be aware that for such writers there are at least two ways forward. One lies in the direction of more explicit and understanding commentary (moving on from "started showing off"); another lies in conveying the nuance of the action and observing it more sharply (something the student may feel freer to do in speech, at this point, than in writing).

Before he can move far in either of these directions, however, this student may well need a more assured control of the mechanics of writing (the secretarial skills) and a more confident sense of his powers as a writer.

So our first job as teachers is to build that confidence by the way we read the story aloud and by a discussion that positively explores its potential. If this gives the writers some pride in their achievements, then there is a chance that — this time or next — they will think the effort to redraft a story is worthwhile. Besides, learning that your story is worth preserving gives a totally new motive for struggling to master "editing" and "secretarial" skills.

A more confident writer

Signs of achievement
Here is another story — to read for enjoyment. You might try reading it aloud, and then noting the things you felt attracted by.

My First Date
My friend and I were sitting down at the Youth club. We were very bored and were just staring at the pictures on the wall.

All of a sudden my eyes caught two girls whom I had not seen before, they were both about John's and my age and were good looking.

Then John gave me a nudge and said, "Have you seen those two girls who have just come in?"

"Yes", I replied.

"Wonder what their names are", I said enquiringly"

"Come on lets find out", was John's answer to that.

John was not very talkative when it came to girls so I could see I was the one who would have to do all the talking on our part. So I started the conversation with the girls by asking them if they wanted a drink, but then I felt a little bit stupid when I saw that they already had drinks. But I pretended not to notice and they replied, "No thanks".

The girls had different coloured hair and one was a little smaller than the other but the both looked the same other wise.

Our first advance on them did not seem to work, so I interupted their conversation once more and asked their names. The taller of the two answered my question.

"My name's Julie and my friend's name is carol, whats your names?"

"My name's Steve and this is John."

Just then the lights in the Youth Club flickered which was the sign that the Youth Club was about to close.

The two girls were just about to leave the the bar, so I asked them if we could walk them home. they both smiled and said "Yes". But as they answered I wondered what I had done, what if they lived miles away, So I quickly said.

"Where do you live?"

Julie answered and said,

"Not far we only live on the Manor".

I felt a bit of relief as it was not too far from where John and I lived.

So we set off from the Youth Club, with the two girls walking in front of us.

Then John asked me which of the girls I liked best, and I replied, "I like both of them",

John replied.

"Well you are not going out with both of them.

"I wish you would not be so daft", I said,

"What I really mean is that I like both of them but I only want to go out with one of them".

I told John to go and ask them if they would go out with us, When he came back, he said they would and we need not choose between them as they had chosen already. I was to go out with Julie.

As we arrived near their homes we left John and Carol because Julie lived on the next road from Carol.

I stood with Julie outside their house and started talking. I asked her which school she went to and all that.

Julie asked me if I was coming out the following night, and I said that John and I would see them at the Youth Club at about half past seven, Julie said, "I will have to go now", so we kissed and she went in.

I met up with John further up the road and we both agreed it was a night well spent.

Let us look first paragraph by paragraph at what this writer is doing.

— evoking a bored mood in a flat style ("just staring");
— playing a cool role, especially via the first comment on John;
— ironically mocking his own social gaffes ("felt a little bit stupid");
— thus sending up "our first advance" and the notion of a campaign;
— tacitly indicating the girls' greater social awareness ("not far") and poise ("we need not choose");
— frankly presenting both boys' lack of sophistication in the conversation on the way home.

This is all very engaging — and also revealing! Steve's interests are very clear: he's looking at himself and John and how they came out of the experience. (It's another story about the way the *boys'* side reacts). As teachers we have to recognise, and respect, the theme he has chosen. Of course there were other themes he might equally well have selected (notably the new relationship with Julie) but that is not what he decides to take on this time. After all, although this is a story that does not commit itself to the complex feelings of a first date, it does leave room for fresh human understanding. In some places Steve is already aware of his own gaucheness; in others, his frank account betrays things that he seems not to have fully understood, and that's a characteristic of this kind of writer.

Some signs of development
If we compare "My First Date" with "The Outcast" it is obvious enough that Steve writes at greater length and has much more control over the mechanics of writing. He has every right to feel more confident within the written medium, but the question is, is he using the relative freedom this gives him to bring new elements of experience into his stories? Let us look first at the texture of a particularly interesting paragraph:

The two girls were just about to leave the the bar, so I asked them if we could walk them home. they both smiled and said "Yes". But as they answered I wondered what I had done, what if they lived miles away, So I quickly said.
"Where do you live?"

Julie answered and said,
"Not far we only live on the Manor".
I felt a bit of relief as it was not too far from where John and I lived.

There are several things going on in such a paragraph. It begins with preparatory action and a brief exchange between Steve and the girls. So far the action is presented as external. Then "as they answered," there is a shift to Steve's inner thoughts, which are not so much reported as dramatised — "what if they lived miles away . . . . "! This momentary inner panic prompts "so I *quickly* said." The opening of Julie's reply — "Not far" — tacitly suggests that she is responding to his feelings. Then, after four quite clipped, tense sentences, comes the more expansive: "I felt a bit of relief as it was not too far from where John and I lived." The rhythm of this sentence enacts a relaxation of tension inside him, and bridges us neatly to the next action, with its confident opening, "So we set off . . . ."

This story, then, is beginning to take on inner thought and feeling, not in isolation but in close relationship to external events. It is beginning to highlight and dwell on certain significant moments: the action conveyed in that paragraph might not take more than five seconds in real time, about as long as it takes to read. (We shall have more to say later about highlights and the way time is handled.)

Learning how to articulate moment by moment experience is a crucial achievement — it affects a lot more than writing stories in school! But there are other ways in which Steve is learning to handle time. If you are into highlights you also have to deal with the space between them. The more you write at length, the more problems this will pose. You have to select when to move on the action. Let's look at Steve doing this:

Our first advance on them did not seem to work, so . . . .
Just then the lights in the Youth Club flickered . . . .
So we set off from the Youth Club . . . .
As we arrived near their homes . . . .
I met up with John further up the road . . . .

These signal to the reader the passing of *relatively* long passages of time — relative, that is, to the sort of paragraph we have just commented on. These two kinds of achievement are complementary, we would say.

Doesn't this throw rather a different light on what we teachers mean by "learning to write a story in paragraphs?" It is clear that this cannot be done to a formula. Until a writer has learnt how to highlight *and* how to signal the passing of relatively long passages of time, two important reasons for paragraph, the mere instruction to "paragraph" can have little or no meaning. Imagine the effect on the writer of "The Outcast," for instance: how would he cope? — what basis is there for paragraphing a story as he currently conceives it?

Interestingly, in several paragraphs towards the end of "My First Date," there is no attempt at close-up. If this were intended to be a story about the beginning of a personal relationship, we might feel disappointed. But the author's perspective on the occasion is more egocentric. What he sees and conveys — especially in three key close-ups — is his own floundering in a new situation where he doesn't know the code. In a sense it's a story against himself that he's telling. The moments he has chosen for close-up confirm that.

Suggestions for a model of development

At this point we want to stand back and ask what we should expect of a theory of writing development. What should it help us to do as teachers? We would like to put forward four provisional answers here.

First, it should help us to look at a piece of writing in a new way, recognising more explicitly what counts as human **experience**. Thus, in "The Outcast" — and many stories like it — the power of the story lies in the cool, amused observation of external behaviour. Such stories do imply quite complex relations and psychological states, but they do so tacitly in the main. Given the text on the page, the reader has a lot of work to do constructing how the characters may be feeling and what they are thinking. ("He wasn't really bothered"). In fact, such stories seem bare and even trite, often enough, until they are animated by an oral rendering (with all that this adds to their meaning).

Moving to "My First Date" and other stories like it, we can see the power of the story moving in new directions. Inner thoughts and feelings are just beginning to be dwelt on and evoked, making important contributions to the significance of certain episodes. Similarly, conversation is beginning to give the flavour at times of the way characters like Steve and John interact. Because of these new elements, personal interactions and psychological events tend to be dealt with more explicitly at times. "It's a change of world," as one of our seminar members once observed.

To sum up, we can ask ourselves, is the story telling us:

— what people are doing, and what is happening to them,
— what they are saying,
— how they are reacting to each other,
— what they are experiencing,
— what they are proposing or anticipating . . .

and is the narrator letting these things speak for themselves or trying to explain why they occur?

Second, it should help us to understand how the writer is dealing with **time.** Experiences in a narrative must happen over time. Thus in both stories the action covers something between half an hour and two or three hours in real time. However, in story time they are over after two or three minutes' reading. What strategies do the two writers make use of to deal with this? Let's look first at some of the key shifts in time that are marked in "The Outcast."

> *After a bit* I told him . . . .
> *Then* I went back over . . . .
> *Then* it was time . . . to go out

Each of these three clauses actually opens a new sentence, instead of starting with his favourite conjunction, "and." That is significant, we take it: the writer has tacitly realised that he is chunking the story into four chronological stages. "After a bit" explicitly indicates that there is a time gap between the previous event and the one about to follow. You could say that "events" have been "omitted"! "Then," on the other hand, could simply indicate one event following another without a time interval: however, on the last occasion at least ("he was blushing then it was time") it seems tacitly to suggest that there is a time gap in the action.

While these four stages represent embryonic episodes, the writer gives minimum emphasis to the chunking or segmenting of time: his story leaves the impression of one continuous flow. No event is highlighted.

Let's look now at "My First Date" and the way time shifts are marked here.

> *All of a sudden* my eyes caught . . . .
> *Then* John gave me a nudge . . . .
> *So I started the conversation* . . . .
> *So I interrupted their conversation once more* . . . .
> *Just then* the lights flickered . . . .
> *So we set off* . . . .
> *Then* John asked me . . . .
> *When he came back* . . . .
> *As we arrived* . . . .
> *I met up* with John . . . .

So far as time is concerned, then, the story is divided into at least eleven chunks. As in "The Outcast" these are chronologically ordered, but the connections seem to be both more varied and more subtle at times.

One reason why there are more chunks, of course, is that the story moves from place to place — and at times does so quickly, leaving us with the sense of time "gap." "So we set off from the Youth Club . . . . As we arrived near their homes . . . I met up with John . . . ." What interests us more, though, are chunks where the writer deliberately seeks to slow down the continuous flow. Take, for example, the chunk that starts with "So I started the conversation." There is no change of place here; instead we are given a quick sequence of events — Steve asks them, sees their drinks, feels stupid, pretends not to notice, and they reply. All this happens in 10-20 seconds, say, in real time: roughly the time it takes you to read it. So the "slowing down" is very considerable — and it has a purpose. For Stephen's story this is a significant **episode**. He opens it with an explicit statement of intention (starting a conversation) and closes with an equally explicit retrospective comment ("*our first advance* on them did not seem to work").

Slowing down is something writers do intuitively — and perhaps later deliberately. This marks a point in the narrative where the episode has special significance for them. We believe that frequently (as in this case) it indicates to us as teachers what the underlying theme is that is preoccupying the writer. So it is really important for teachers to be aware of these highlighted episodes, otherwise they might inadvertently misconstrue the main interest of the story.

We have called this kind of episode a **highlight,** borrowing a term from another art, and we'll say more about this in the fourth section. For the moment, the important thing is the difference in the way time is handled.

To sum up, we can ask ourselves:

— has the writer, consciously or not, given the impression of a continuous flow of time (and for what purposes)?

— which chunks of time has it seemed appropriate to sketch in quickly?

— which chunks have been significant enough to dwell on, thus slowing down story time?

— has a chronological sequence seemed appropriate, or have there been reasons for changing the time order?

Third, it should help us to appreciate the significance of **context** — the background details of people, setting or era. Your personal stories usually include people you already know and settings you are familiar with; they are set in an era of time you take for granted. But your reader is not necessarily in the know, so as you construct your story what strategies do you use to fill out the "context" for the action — the things you already know and the reader doesn't?

Let us look at the way each writer deals with these matters. "The Outcast," for instance, opens by "introducing us" (as we say) to the main character. In fact this is the purpose of the first five clauses — a kind of embryonic paragraph. We are told about Les's age, where he works, and how he visits his gran every week. On the surface these seem to be pretty bald facts, but what might the writer feel they imply? Although he doesn't think it necessary to fill this out for the reader, we might well be expected to gather things like this:

— I'm very friendly with a boy who's older than me and he's out at work too, not in school (you might say he's quite a hero);

— he's a family boy, he likes his gran (and he isn't above playing with someone who's still at school).

That's one way of introducing character: it is a very typical generic choice for a writer at this developmental stage, we feel. Of course it tells us that Les is going to be thematically important. Everything else we learn about him is given through his actions (and refusals to act!)

In "My First Date," John is introduced by a different strategy:

My friend and I were sitting . . . .
about John's and my age . . . .
"Come on lets find out," was John's answer . . . .
John was not very talkative . . . .
not too far from where John and I lived . . . .

Now we could translate this as: "I have got a friend and his name is John. He's interested in girls but he is not very talkative with them. He lives round near me and he is about my age and we go to the Youth Club together and one night we went . . . ." But this would imply that John was central to the story. Instead, what Steve does is to introduce details about his friend gradually, at appropriate moments, and sometimes explicitly, sometimes by implication. So "character introduction," in this case, is integrated into the body of the story.

These are two strategies — two generic choices — each useful for a different purpose. If you can handle both, you have a better repertoire to draw on when writing further stories. Perhaps we should point out, in passing, that when it comes to the other two characters, Julie and Carol, Steve changes his strategy, attempting to fit in a "cameo" description — and, as it happens, it doesn't come off! However, in "The Outcast" we get no further than "the girl."

Exactly the same kind of options can be taken up for **setting** (and **era**). As it happens, neither of these writers thinks the setting important — their interests are elsewhere! But, of course, it is quite common for young writers to take a setting like "the baths" or "the Youth Club" for granted. All we would point out at this stage is that, when it does appear, setting often comes in a descriptive chunk, though it is equally possible — as we shall see in a later piece — to integrate it into the line of action.

To sum up, then, let us ask ourselves:

— how aware is the writer of the need to fill out the context for characters, setting or era (as appropriate)?
— how elementary or flexible are the strategies s/he uses to introduce or develop background details that s/he knows and the reader doesn't?
— what is the significance of the background details s/he does introduce (and are the implications clear to readers)?

Fourth, it should help us appreciate in what ways — and to what degree — various **elements** in the story are **integrated.**

So far we have talked of **experience, time** and **context** separately; this is partly a matter of analytic convenience, partly an appropriate response to the pieces we have dealt with so far. In concluding this section we want to suggest that there already are forms of **integration** in both pieces, and that in writers at a further stage of development — as we shall be seeing — integration will be more sophisticated still.

To begin with let us go back to the episode in "My First Date" where Steve highlights "our first advance." As he slows down the story time, he makes room to include internal thought and feeling alongside external behaviour: he asks a question, sees they already have drinks, feels a bit stupid, pretends not to notice . . . . For a moment, there is a new kind of density to experience. This integrated ebb-and-flow between action, speech, inner thought and reaction (leading to further spoken interplay) begins to feel like the *texture* of actual lived-through experience.

As these two processess of "highlighting" and "integration" continue in the "episode" that follows, it seems that the writer is offering more complex signals on which the reader's construction can be based. We can now make a distinction between thoughts being *stated* and *dramatised* — the signals of panic have more impact on the reader in the latter case ("what if they lived miles away"!) Similarly feelings (of relief) may not only be stated but enacted to some degree in the relaxed rhythm of a sentence like "I felt a bit of relief as it was not too far . . . ." By comparison, many sentences of "The Outcast" — especially "he wasn't reraly Bothered about the Girl So we went home" — leave the reader to construct some potential feeling not specifically signalled in the text: this writer has still to learn how to use rhythm and dramatic expression to shape and communicate the quality of inner thoughts and feelings.

These are fairly advanced forms of integration, it seems. In a less advanced writer we might be excited, as teachers, to see dialogue emerging as a way of indicating character and relationships in association with external behaviour and action. This is what happens as the boys follow the girls home in "My First Date," and it is something we might be hoping for as a new development in the writer of "The Outcast."

Equally in more advanced stories we shall be seeing more complex forms of integration. Thus, apparently background details in the setting become symbolic of a prevailing mood of calm or foreboding, for example. Or, by evoking memories and fantasy projections, the writer will bring events from various chunks of time into new and complex relationships.

To sum up then, we can ask ourselves:

— is dialogue beginning to indicate character and interplay between people?
— is the writer integrating what people are doing with what they are thinking and feeling?
— are thoughts and feelings beginning to be dramatised and enacted, thus revealing the motives for external events?
— what further and more complex forms of integration are emerging?

Diagnosing constraints on story construction

Let us now turn to the negative comments about "The Outcast" with which we began; can we use these positively and diagnostically to understand potential difficulties that may be facing many writers at a similar staging point in development?

In presenting himself and his friend, the writer, consciously or not, has had to dig into background knowledge that he normally takes for granted. From the mass of such knowledge he has quickly had to unearth, select and order, two, three, four, five ... details about Les which will help the reader to start the process of imagining his friend. Then, from the complex ebb and flow of a longish experience he has had to recall certain key events, summon up some vivid images from his memory, and construct these into a story form which gives him and his readers an amused insight into Les's behaviour — in this case. In oral story-telling he could give his whole attention to this and, for all we know, might well be able to carry on all of these mental processes with ease. In fact, he might be so relaxed that he could, at the same time, feed on his audience's responses and try progressively to involve them more deeply, discovering new possibilities in the story he was telling.

In writing, however, he faces new problems. It's hardly likely that ten years of schooling have left him unaware that in the eyes of many people he is failing to control capitals, punctuation, paragraphing and other more complex features. So as such writers sit down to write the story, instead of the handwritten forms coming out semi-automatically with little or no further attention, there may be anxious interruption of story construction, every word or two, when they consciously turn to ask themselves — what is the lower case form? — what is the spelling pattern? — should there be a full stop? What's more, in such cases, if the act of writing is at all laborious and time consuming, the process of story construction may be slowed down so much that what was going to come next is forgotten; and if reading is not fluent, story construction is again severely interrupted whenever the writer looks back to check what s/he has said in the story so far.

To sum up: wherever there is slowness in reading, laborious handwriting, anxiety and insecurity over control of spelling and capitalisation, confusion over the need for punctuation, the extra cognitive attention demanded must inevitably act as a brake on the vital processes of story construction.

How do many undeveloped writers cope with such problems? We suggest that they draw on the most accessible and elementary side of their linguistic repertoire: simple and accessible vocabulary; simple and repetitive patterns of clauses. And secondly, they keep to a sequence of external events perhaps, avoiding the need to interweave spoken words, inner thought and feelings, or narrator's comments, into the body of their text. If we are right, this explains a good deal of what is happening in "The Outcast." The promising sign is that, in this case, a simpler story has emerged triumphantly — so far as this writer is concerned. In fact, the best story he wrote that year!

What we would really like to know is what kinds of stories this boy would have told and recorded on tape given the right encouragement and setting. Then, given the chance to use such tapes, what potentialities in written story-telling might be opened up?

In "My First Date," by contrast, there seems to be a relatively assured control of spelling, capitals, punctuation, paragraphing, a wider vocabulary, and more complex sentence structures. For much of the time these appear semi-automatic. Only occasionally, when dialogue and narrative have to be integrated and paragraphed, does the automatic control slip momentarily, producing an error at a very low level, such as a lower case for "carol." Interestingly, at other points, the writer's sense of balance between clauses suggests he might introduce semi-colons into his repertoire, to indicate sentence rhythms in a more refined way (see his second paragraph).

What can we learn from this as teachers?
It seems vital, then, in the early lessons with a class to observe writers closely. Assuming they have found something they really want to write about:

- — what is the speed of their handwriting?
- — how long do they take to complete a line, or page?
- — how many breaks of attention do we note in the course of a sentence?
- — what signs of anxiety are there over spelling?
- — does their written vocabulary seem simpler than their spoken (perhaps suggesting a search for words they are secure in spelling)?
- — when they read their work aloud, do they read fluently with a sense of meaning in their voice, or is their intonation flat and without any dramatic modulation?
- — how long do they take to read a page silently?
- — when they edit their writing, what difficulties do they find?

CHAPTER 2

A wider circle of social experience

With younger students it is natural to expect family and friends to loom large in their personal stories. In early adolescence, as we have seen, girl-friends or boy-friends begin to enter, alongside the earlier relationships. But with the increasing self-consciousness of adolescence — already present in the first two stories — such experiences are often felt to be too private, perhaps, and that source for personal stories begins to fade. At precisely the same time, however, older students are becoming involved in a wider range of encounters, as they begin to take on new social roles — joining and helping to run clubs, getting involved in voluntary work, taking a part-time job, baby-sitting and looking after younger children, visiting or helping out with sick and elderly relatives ("up to his Gran's every week"), taking part in political activities . . . . Some schools largely ignore these changing experiences, others actively extend them.

Among English teachers there has been a tendency to treat personal stories primarily as the "cherishing of private souls," as Dorothy and Douglas Barnes (1983) have pointed out. If it's not confessional, it counts for less! But schools or colleges that are aware of that widening circle of social activity and encounters are exploring new purposes for writing. Readers may want to be informed by a story as well as to enjoy it. So the range broadens out from personal stories or diaries to narrative reports or accounts, based on participant-observer experiences.

In this broader sense, personal "stories" still have an enormous amount to offer. The power of narrative keeps you in touch with the ebb and flow of felt experience. At the same time it leaves room for you to construct, interpret, criticise and reflect on the meaning of fresh social experience as you encounter it.

Besides, these new social roles often move beyond the security of the known, and — at a moment of relative vulnerability — test your knowledge, your social poise, your judgement, your ability to act independently (and to seek help at appropriate moments). You may have every need to reflect, to struggle with emotional problems and adjustments, to get some common sense perspective on yourself and the others involved, and equally to recognise what count as achievements and successes. So writing can serve valuable purposes if you need to take stock. What's more, you may well have a natural readership among your peers, all keen to learn more about things they also are just on the threshold of experiencing — or are seriously considering.

So far as the teacher is concerned there are important choices of form to suggest. If the experience is likely to be disturbing, baffling or upsetting, then a diary or journal — to which a teacher is given privileged access — may be most valuable; if the experience is easier to cope with, or as it is brought under control and a sense of confidence emerges, a narrative report for a specific readership may be an appropriate choice. So much is possible between these poles that we have to be selective here, offering just three examples of the ways ahead.

An elementary narrative report

We begin with a narrative account by a fourteen year-old who has been involved in visiting a local Infants School, reading a selection of books to a group of children, noting their reactions, and producing a story of his own to read to them.[1] What might his readers — in a similar class preparing a visit the following year — stand to gain from his account? Further, what has he gained himself by writing up the experience? Let's look, again, for the signs of positive achievement as we read it aloud.

When we first went down to the school we read the children a selection of stories written by other authors. The kids were then asked what story they wanted us to write for them, subjects ranged from witches to submarines from wild animals to army boats.

the context is sketched in (read . . . a selection . . . by other authors!)

A lad called David Watt asked me to write him a story on wild animals so I started off with a Fonz like lion called Vince and a group of other way-out animal characters but that turned out as a mistake so I scrapped that story and got down to writing an entirely new story with an entirely new plot with entirely new characters.

a sense of direct contact with the writer and his struggles (a lad called David . . . scrapped that . . . off again)

cheerful exaggeration of his plight (entirely . . . entirely . . . entirely!)

So I started off again and came up with four new characters a Rabbit called Carrots Conway a Pig called Porky a Wolf called Will Wolf Esq and a duck called Devious, then the main problem was fitting them into the story and giving them an individual character which appears to be original.

concrete particulars about story and its problems

Another problem I faced was time, as the first story I had written had taken me 2 weeks approx there was little time to start the story as I had to get quite a lot of work done in a short space of time.

So the story was done in time and the lad seemed to like it and thought it was very good . . . .

When we returned to the school we went to our appropriate groups and read the books to them and got ready to takes notes on what they thought of them. The general opinion to them was good, all four kids listened to each story as well as them being told to them individually.

I have learned that writing a childrens book is not an easy task. First of all they are of an entirely different age to you so you have to cast your mind back to when you were their age and remember what you liked about stories. I also learnt that if a young child has set his heart on a book on say dinosaurs then you will have to move heaven and earth to persuade him to listen to the story.

Mind you it is very easy to write a story if the child you are writing for has given you a subject to work on in my case Wild Animals.

Judicious summing up of what "I have learned" all directly and confidently addressing reader: ("mind you")

This lad comes over as a character. He's obviously enjoyed the experience — and he's enjoyed writing this. It's a real story — almost a blow by blow account as he grapples with his animal story. You feel in touch with his struggles. He's earned the confidence to draw his own conclusions — and he's got a real sense of being in conversation with you, the reader, as he sums up.

What empowers this writer is the interest he's generated in the experience itself, the new confidence of seeing himself as an "author," the belief that he has learnt something himself, and that he has worthwhile advice to pass on. So he writes with a personal voice and a strong sense of a real audience who'll want to know.

We feel pretty certain that, in this case, it is the teaching context that has released a new potential in him.[2] He has not been rushed into an impersonal, objective stance — so often imposed unthinkingly in school — and as a result there is a valuable sense of control and discovery.

Diagnosing the new demands on the writer
A narrative such as we have just looked at seems to start as a personal story (involving "us") but ends up passing on socially useful knowledge. It's a kind of bridge between the two — valuable both in itself and as a transition phase for the writer. By the end he is beginning to see how his experience ("in my case") may

represent something typical. In part it's an instance for a type of experience that may be met by others, he guesses.[3]

There seem to be five kinds of demand that this writer has to deal with in structuring this account:

a) The enterprise extends over several weeks, so he has to make a ruthless selection of the chunks of time he wants to include in his narrative.

b) The encounter in the primary school is a joint experience planned and undertaken with some of his classmates. Thus "When we first went down to the school" . . . . "When we returned to the school." Both these paragraphs are dealt with less personally.

c) The writing of the animal story in the time between the visits is dealt with personally and there is a slight problem in welding it to the first visit. (It would have been better if his second paragraph had begun "A lad called David Watt had asked me . . . .")
The movement from a joint experience and back sets up an ambiguity whether the main narrative perspective should derive from "we" or "I."

d) The general lessons he draws from this experience are easiest to cope with as an addendum, and he does decide to construct an ending of this kind ("I have learnt," "I also learnt," "Mind you, it is very easy"), handling its construction with assurance.

e) As he reports the writing of the animal story, however, some of the events seem to him to illustrate "problems" that he wants to mention to the reader — implied warnings for next year's students, if you like. So in the middle of the narrative sequence he interpolates "the main problem was . . ." and "Another problem I faced was . . ." Both problems are dealt with successfully, but when he returns to the narrative line — "So the story was done" — he doesn't quite find an appropriate conjunction.

To sum up, there are new questions for the teacher and students to take into account as they review the possibilities of such a report:

— as the enterprise may cover several weeks, which incidents should be selected (how is the time to be "chunked")?

— where individual and joint enterprise is involved, how best can incidents that are individual be linked up with those that are collaborative (a form of "integration")?

— where do the lessons to be drawn arise from particular yet typical experience (and thus need to be interpolated into the narrative, perhaps); where do they arise from general reflections?

— in general, how best can the writer contextualise the experience, taking into account potential readers who are not in the know?

Moving into a more complex account

Our next account is from an older student reporting on her experience of helping people in a mental hospital — an experience she found difficult and challenging. In this case, her complete report runs to rather over 5,000 words. Let us start by looking at the opening chapter which tells us how she became involved.

Structuring a report in chapters sets up new questions — how is she going to use the introductory chapter? Let's look at it with positive achievements in mind.

The Volunteer

Some of the volunteers who go and help at Hollymoor belong to an organisation known as the League of Friends or W.R.V.S. who provide valuable supporting services. Others are men and women who do not belong to any organisation; I myself come under this category.

I first became involved in community service about five and a half months ago, when at school. Mrs. Long a teacher asked who would be interested in doing something different than games on a Monday afternoon. She called it community service, she herself belonged to the League Of Friends and had found it a rewarding experience.

A meeting was held and she explained that sixth formers in the past had gone to hospitals, schools, old peoples homes etc to go and help once a week instead of doing games. Its not that I don't like games I thoroughly enjoy playing rounders and going swimming but I felt I wanted to help some one and it would be a very interesting experience. My ambition is to become a nurse and to visit a mental hospital regularly intrigued me.

I don't know what I expected because I'd never been to a mental hospital and only had a short stay in a normal hospital, so I didn't have any ideas what it was going to be like. When thinking about it I could easily imagine dark, cold cells with massive padlocks on the barred doors to keep the patients in!

Another girl in my year (Dawn) also wanted to visit a hospital. So we were sorted out to go to 'Hollymoor Hospital, Northfield.'

The other pupils were organised to go and help at near by schools to help the children learn to read.

I was looking forward to next Monday with an open mind!

This is a writer who is conscious of a role she can fulfill with respect to a group of readers who are no better informed than she was when she started. Thus, right from the start she is assuming the need to sketch in background information. We can imagine a sequence of questions in her mind — what's a volunteer? — how do you volunteer? — why did you volunteer? — what did you think you were volunteering for? There is something very poised and rational about that sequencing.

The interesting thing, however, is that instead of giving a set of factual answers, she chooses to tell the story of how "I first became involved," and she retraces it again, as it happened — as if ignorant of the outcome. This cleverly allows her to record her feelings at the time, interwoven with the socially organised events:

Mrs. Long a teacher asked . . .
A meeting was held . . .

I felt I wanted to help someone
. . .

to visit a mental hospital . . .
intrigued me . . .

I didn't know what I expected
. . .

I could easily imagine . . .

We were sorted out . . .
The other pupils were organised . . .

. . . looking forward . . . with an open mind!

Like an expert story-teller she plays on her readers' imagination ("dark, cold cells with massive padlocks") and their sense of expectation as they look forward with her to "next Monday."

Part of the power of the story is its ability to engage readers imaginatively, to draw them into the events alongside the participants. But this writer has further purposes in mind — to instruct and inform us, let us say. Her work in this chapter is a valuable reminder for us teachers that reports do not always have to be impersonal, factual and cold. This writer is able to move very flexibly between, on the one hand, the personal and social knowledge gained in the course of her experience, and, on the other, the interest, foreboding and uncertainties she felt at the time. The knowledge she has gained cannot help but give her (now) a different kind of confidence in telling her story (then).

Some further demands on the writer

On first reading, there is a deceptive simplicity about this piece of writing. After reflection, one realises some of the complex shifts that the writer has to negotiate. The basic problem is how to integrate social knowledge into a personal account. A key decision, we believe, was taken when the title for the chapter was selected: "The Volunteer" proposes a theme that places the narrator within a wider social category. Two things follow. First, she is able to use her experience as typical — as typifying what *might* often happen (as well as narrating what *did* happen). Second, she can incorporate information about other volunteers, including a definition of sub-groups (League of Friends, W.R.V.S.) within the overall social category of "voluntary" or "community" service.

The title helps, then, and the interweaving of commentary and background information within the narrative "plot" is deftly carried through on the whole. It is important to realise, though, that she is having to control shifts from casual comments ("Its not that I don't like games") to more formal and impersonal statements ("a meeting was held"); from detached, informative uses of language ("Some of the volunteers . . . belong . . . Others are . . .") to emotive phrases that dramatise inner feelings ("I could easily imagine . . .").

Integrating such things within the paragraph is a much tougher agenda than adding the social information as an addendum, on the lines of the previous writer, say. (It's not surprising, then, that at one point in the third paragraph, her competent control of punctuation momentarily breaks down).

To sum up, wherever there is an extended enterprise and report, teacher and students may need to discuss at length beforehand:

— the possible needs and interests of readers (with real questions being directed to the writer — how did you feel? What happened then? Why did you? . . .);
— which chain of incidents to select and whether to organise these into chapters or sections;
— what unifying themes to explore in order to integrate the material within a chapter;
— how to recall and dramatise personal feelings and responses while you were engaged in a socially organised sequence of events;
— where best to interpolate within the narrative both advice and the social knowledge that was gained;
— how to draft, and to enlist peers and other readers in giving valuable response to the draft and advice on re-drafting.

Coming to terms with social pressures

Going into a mental hospital, and many other social experiences like it, is liable to drop students out of their depth at some moment. When that occurs, if students do want to write about it, there is a different purpose for writing — and a different kind of reader is needed. The writer may want a chance to disentangle confused and painful feelings, to place the experience as a past event and, from a retrospective position, to begin to evaluate it. This suggests a sympathetic reader who is personally trusted, rather than a wider public audience.

On such occasions a diary or personal journal offers writers a chance to write for themselves rather than have to take the needs of readers too much into account, and leaves them free to construct whatever form they wish, to follow the contours of their day. In the example that follows, the writer produced a fully developed narrative — rather than a set of jottings, for example, about her first day's work experience in a hairdresser's. What she does in the process is worth looking at closely.

Day I: Monday 19th October

I entered through the large glass doors. It was ten to nine, at least I was early! I dreaded the thought of being late on my very first day, I felt excited about the event, but very apprehensive. I felt clean and in my opinion, very smart, I hoped that the employer felt that too. I was given a locker, for my coat and valuables, and then was taken into the hairdressing department. It was immaculately clean and extremely tidy. The floor shone, it seemed a pity that hair would be dropped all over it, and customers with their dirty feet would tread over it too. Still thats inevitable in this type of profession I continually re-iterated to myself. The walls were papered with a bright pattern of very green and yellow flowers, set on a white background. The bright green chairs were neatly tucked away making the scene attractive. It all seemed so very fresh.

The manageress, Sue, introduced me to the hairdressers. The nervousness had eased off, as I was made very welcome.

First Sue asked me if I could wash hair properly. I told her, being truthful, that I wasn't very sure.

She explained and demonstrated how to wash hair. It looked quite easy, so I thought

I watched the apprentices wash client's hair, recording all their actions. My unwished for moment had arrived, I had to wash somebody's hair.

In my mind I tried to recollect the demonstration given. Oh what the hell! I'd say to myself. I would have to have done it sometime anyway.

I began to wash Janice, a hairdresser's hair, making sure that my actions were correct, I thought my first attempt was pretty successful. Neverthless, as I was washing Janice's hair, Sue asked me to wash the client's hair sitting beside Janice. Agreeing with her, I said I would when I had finished washing Janice's hair.

I didn't rush and finish Janice's hair quickly as I imagined that would complicate things and besides that I might get it wrong. Not deliberately trying to be slow either, I continued with what I was doing.

Two minutes after Sue had given me instructions she came out and told me off for being slow. She explained that if I wanted to do hairdressing I'd have to put my skates on and work faster.

I was unavoidably at the fact that as I had only been there for an hour and that there was no necessity to tell me off for something I was in the process of learning. Still, never mind, Sally! I repeated to myself.

It would get better as the day went on, I hoped!

I stood in the corner of the shop gazing into mid-air, I was thinking about the incident earlier. It was playing on my mind, it disturbed me, I didn't like it!

I came to my senses when Heather, an apprentice, approached me with a message from Sue saying that I wasn't to stand in the corner "doing nothing" but to watch the hair stylists, as I made the shop look untidy. Obeying her instructions I helplessly watched the hair stylist.

I was studyng Dawn, a stylist, she was doing a perm. The curlers were neatly put into the lady's hair and then the perm lotion was put over her scalp. The lotion had to be left on for a short period of time. So as to keep the client occupied I was to get some magazines nearby. Doing so I walked over to the magazines and gave them to the client.

Sue called me to and told me to pick my feet up and stop dragging them across the floor. This was the limit! I felt a great deal of resentment for Sue. I was now very self-pitying, because I had tried so desperately hard to give a good first impression.

I was told that my lunch break would be from twelve to twelve-thirty, but later on was informed that it was to be altered from two to two-thirty. After my half hour dinner break I returned promptly to help tidy up the salon as we were to travel up to London for a stylist competition. I was given warning beforehand so my family knew I'd be late home.

We arrived in London at five, half an hour before the competition began It was held in a large shop. While it was taking place we, the spectators, were shown around the shop's 'Disneyland'. Returning to find the results, we discovered we hadn't won.

We arrived back home at nine-forty p.m. I was dropped off near my house, which I was pleased about. My mum greeted me and asked what it was like. I told her it was a great disappointment. She again asked me whether I liked it, I retorted "I don't think I do, I just don't think I do!"

What is narrative helping her to do here? She is revisiting and, we feel, reliving some of the key events in detail. Having entered "through the large glass doors," she dwells moment by moment on the new experience. A guarded sense of relief — "at least I was early" — cancels earlier moments of "dread." There's a conflict of excitement and apprehension. Her confidence was bolstered, she remembers, as she felt clean and smart. Next moment there's a naive sense of wonder, almost enchantment, at the shining floor, the immaculate cleanliness. She's caught and responds to the "very green and yellow flowers" of the wallpaper and the neatly tucked-away green chairs. All "so very fresh."

This is a dramatic re-enactment of encountering a new world. The heightened awareness and sensitiveness of these early minutes is symptomatic (and, later, significant too). However, from this point she is caught in a see-saw of events:

EXTERNAL ACTION	INNER THOUGHTS AND FEELINGS
made very welcome . . .	
	being truthful, ... I wasn't very sure.
explained and demonstrated . . .	it looked quite easy . . .
	My unwished for moment had arrived . . .
	Oh, what the hell! I'd say to myself . . .
making sure that my actions were correct . . .	. . . pretty successful . . .
I didn't rush . . .	
she came out and told me off . . .	I might get it wrong.

A passsage like this reveals how procedures that might seem routine and second nature to some people cost her a constant effort to keep under control. She struggled to cope (she remembers) but the social tension and lack of understanding progressively demoralised her.

What's really interesting is the way she looks back, exploring the pattern of her reactions to events:

> . . . there was no necessity to tell me off . . . .
> Still, never mind, Sally! I repeated to myself. It would get better . . . .
> It was playing on my mind, it disturbed me, I didn't like it! . . . .
> I helplessly watched . . . .
> This was the limit! I felt a great deal of resentment . . . .
> I was now very self-pitying, because I had tried so desperately hard . . . .

By the end of the morning she has undergone all this: it is a demanding and unnerving experience. The fact that she can later record it so honestly, analysing her feelings and thoughts like this, is quite remarkable for a fifteen year-old. (Small wonder that the excursion to London is not highlighted and is so briefly sketched in: it might have been the central social experience of the day, with all its excitement — but that wasn't to be).

The quality of writing suggests someone who is not trying to slide over very unpleasant experiences, who wants to some degree to face (and present)the truth. It is a very important reason for writing about social experiences that are difficult.

To sum up, then, wherever students face difficulties in new social experiences, teachers will need to ask themselves:

— how to turn these difficulties and a sense of failure into a positive learning experience;
— how to encourage recall of, and even elicit, the texture of difficult moments so that honest evaluations become possible;
— how to encourage writers to stand back and retrospectively comment on their present understanding of past feelings and actions.

When does narrative particularise, when does it typify?

In the first section of this book we have seen narrative moving in two fundamental directions. These arise from the nature of personal and social experience itself.

Social life constantly falls into habitual patterns and routines. We go up to the baths every week. At the weekend we go to see our gran. These repeated patterns run through our day too. They are shaped by the culture we live in. Even the events that feel unique and personal to us — like being watched by a girl at the baths, making a first date, or volunteering for community service — are representative of many other people's experiences in our culture. They are part of larger patterns that many young people will follow in their life story.

So there are two general kinds of interest people can have in writing or reading about personal experiences. We can be interested in the **particularities,** in the unique impact of the lived-through experience on an individual person. Equally, we can be interested in what is **typical,** in what the story tells us we may repeatedly or regularly expect to find. The difference is clearly discernible; but the two interests are by no means incompatible.

Thus, while telling her readers the story of her own volunteering, a writer can be well aware that she is one of a group, and that there are procedures and routines that all of them will experience and have to learn. If the writer's purpose is to inform and advise a reader, then she will naturally want to emphasise typical patterns and routines — even typical patterns of feelings and expectations. Writers may even feel that an incident they have experienced or witnessed points to a general human truth: "I also learnt that if a young child has set his heart on say dinosaurs then you will have to move heaven and earth to persuade him to listen" to anything else!

However, these tendencies to perceive patterns, typical routines, generalised "truths" (as we call them) arise from particular events, each involving individuals in a unique social network. David Watt asked for a story on wild animals: other requests "ranged from witches to submarines." The strength of personal narrative is that it preserves (in part at least) the writer's sense that this was a unique occasion and s/he actually lived through it.

If your whole interest lies in perceiving, exploring or celebrating the experience as unique, your focus as a writer is primarily on its particularity, moment by moment. For the girl who went to work at the hairdresser's, the experience — and it gets worse as the week goes on — is too painful to allow her at this stage to recognise and think about the general structures of power, or of insensitive authority in a workplace. She reads the experience as unique and personal. But it is also possible for us as readers, if we wish, to perceive typicality, the commonality of experience, in what went on. (And that's how teachers felt when Les "wasn't really bothered," or Julie and Carol chose who they were going out with. "Just like kids at our school," they said.)

A pedagogic failure of the past has been for us teachers of English to concentrate so exclusively on personal narratives that explore the unique and inner world — "cherishing private souls" — that we have been unaware of, or excluded, the power of narrative for other purposes. Ironically, there have been recurrent mistakes when "What I did at Christmas," "My School Holidays," and a whole array of similar assignments produced not vividly particular moments but crude sterotypes.

The power of personal narrative, when it is used to inform, advise and instruct, derives from the writer's ability to keep both fundamental interests in play: the sense of a unique, lived-through experience, and the awareness of recurring patterns and typicality. Accounts that typify in impersonal, general terms, on the other hand, may lose their human interest by their very abstraction. We have seen this again, and again in written character studies based on literary texts,[4] and equally in sociological studies. From the point of view of English teaching then, there is still a great deal to be explored in the potential range of personal narratives.

CHAPTER 3

Imaginary stories

Why invent fictions?

When we tell a story about our personal lives, we don't always tell it as it is — do we? We'd like to have felt bigger than we were, to have been braver, less bashful, more witty . . . . Or we have made such a fool of ourselves that we play up our stupidity. We brag about our father or mother, we heap coals of fire on Uncle Walter. "My mum had a terrible operation," "My dad won the war." It certainly makes a better story if he did. From a very early age we learn to romanticise our personal lives and fly off into fiction.

How do we do it so easily? However young we are, we're bound to have tried on a whole wardrobe of fictional (and romantic) selves. Isn't it nice to be a rabbit, a Fonz-like lion or a devious Duck? (We have no difficulty in throwing off naturalism — dragons, ogres, dwarfs, giants, witches and wizards, we try on the lot). But we also like to be bus drivers or shop keepers, to keep house and have parties, to take toy dogs to the vet or to be the doctor coming to examine the baby: there's a streak of realistic interest in such fantasies, too. And for a bit of excitement, let's be cowboys on the trail, space travellers, or the builders of secret dens and fortresses. At that age we *act out* all these fantasies — in the playground, in the street, anywhere. They make up half our lives, so is it any wonder that we project them into stories about our "real" selves?

This is another human propensity, and it doesn't wither away, whatever adults pretend. It may all go underground into the private fantasies of adolescence and "mature years," the comforting day-dream or the nightmares that oppress us with their intense "reality." Look at the compulsive urge to keep feeding these inner fictions night after night in the imaginary worlds of television — or of cinema, the theatre and books. They seem to be inextricably woven into our lives, whether to help us make sense of day to day reality, or to escape from it.

Of course, compared with children you don't see so many adults making up "fictional" stories and telling them to each other. Telling jokes in a pub, perhaps, or stories round a campfire. Not making a regular habit of it, though. Perhaps it is

28

something to do with our society and culture — think of the medieval world by comparison.

Is it to do with "shades of the prison house"? To create characters with their own lives in an imaginary world you need to shake off "getting and spending": it demands sustained time and energies. We have only to observe young children at play to realise how much of both they invest.

However, there *is* one place within our culture where time can be made, and that is in school, within the English and Drama lessons. But then the question is: to what purpose?

Why write imaginary stories?

Inevitably personal experience is limited. We have curiosities or longings to imagine what might have happened, if our lives had taken a different turn.

And among the experiences that memory constantly draws us back to are some where we wish we *had* acted differently. Imagination is frequently under pressure from such feelings.

There are other things in our own lives we don't want to face up to, and certainly not to tell others. By imaginative projection we can sometimes explore them under the cloak of fiction. This can be done in earnest, but it can also be done through comedy. The laughter may hurt, but perhaps not as much.

There are other moments when our imaginations are captivated by worlds very different to ours — admiration, enchantment, fascination, seduction and even repulsion will draw us into them. They test possibilities in ourselves we hadn't dreamt of: but now we can, if we dare.

These are stories for ourselves, feeding our own personal needs. But there is another group of stories that we invent for others, to put a point of view, draw a moral lesson, instruct, persuade or warn. They are part of a long tradition of parables, allegories, fables, satirical sketches, morality plays, documentary "dramas" — and nowadays, advertising fictions.

These are just some of the reasons for creating a new central character — or maybe a group of characters? — and for working to develop new settings and construct new plots. Right through to 16 many pupils are encouraged by their English teachers to do precisely that, presumably because the teacher has an inkling that there is scope here for special kinds of learning.

Achievements in an elementary story

Once again, we want to start by reading a story, with a commitment to bringing out the best in it. Remember that you are looking at an optimum achievement of this young writer. As you render it aloud, what positive signs of building and entering an imaginary world begin to strike you? (It will help if you cover up the comments, first time round).

Been Shot in the War

I was walking just around the camp ———— straight into the action
when suddenly I fell down.

I did not feel anything, and then I
went to a sleep.

Next I knew I was on a stretcher and
soldiers were looking at me and Saying, ———— a sense of dazed confusion on a
'keep him warm and etc". I opened my stretcher
eyes one of the soldiers told that I had
been shot.

I asked if, it was bad and one of them
said, Yes it is bad you have been shot in ———— gradually becoming more aware
the throat." The Nurse told me to take it of details
easy becase I could not talk yet. So when
the Sergeant went, the nurse tidied my
bed and she went out. I started to think metaphoric force of "feeling
about my wife and the other soldiers cold inside" (glimpsing death as
that were not lucky and I was. I felt cold ———— possible)
inside as the room getting cold, and
colder I thought what would have
happened if I was dead. After awhile the contrast between doctor's
doctor came and the nurse came in and ———— jollying and his pain
the doctor told me that I was fine and he
would have to take the bullet out and ———— a natural fade-out
then maybe I can go home. I felt the
pain in the neck as if something was
stunging me.

Then I went to sleep.
I slept for a long time.

Skilfully read, this story achieves the sense of being taken unawares by the sudden shock of something not fully comprehended, of disorientation, of gradual recovery — beginning to piece together the bare essentials of what's happened. A camp, a stretcher, a sergeant, a nurse . . . . all get a mention but none is elaborated. The actual focus is on the moment when the narrator lies alone in a room getting colder and colder. This changes the quality of the story. It slows up momentarily, as if everything has become still after the sporadic activity. It's what Joyce might have called an "epiphanic moment," very simply suggesting things of deeper significance, "my wife . . . the other soldiers . . . if I was dead." A good moment to contemplate together in class, when the story is read aloud.

Scope for special kinds of learning?

In reading such a story, and in discussing it with a group or with the class, what are we hoping for? Again, it would be easy to dismiss this story (especially because of awkwardnesses that arise as the writer struggles with English as her second language). The point we want to make is that such stories, elementary as they are, are a potential foundation for the class to penetrate further into an imaginary world. Shock, pain, bewilderment, dread . . . these are the key experiences the writer is focussing on. We have all had them — to some degree — but can we relate them to this extreme situation, and articulate how it might feel? This is the challenge she has begun to take on, and not surprisingly it is making very great demands on her.

Can we help her — and help the rest of the class (and ourselves) — to build on this imaginary exploration? We might try:

- to collect and register the perceptions she's already offered, making this man and his situation credible and "real" (so we all begin to "suspend disbelief");
- to take the experience of lying on a stretcher, perhaps, hearing fragments of speech and build up a sound collage (on tape?);
- moving into role, to imagine his stream of consciousness as he begins slowly to realise what being shot in the throat could portend;

and in ways like these to allow room for complexity and understanding of the experience to develop.

What is so good about this story is that it sets us off, so economically, in the right directions. It asks us to imagine what it must have been like for this man, in these moments. It begins to take us into his inner consciousness. It draws on experiences common to all of us but demands that we try to project them into an alien, extreme situation. That is why, we would say, such stories are worth taking further and why they offer the opportunity for a special kind of learning.

A more confident writer

Signs of achievement
Like our first example, the next story takes the narrator through an experience that is alien and extreme. It's worth reading slowly to get the full impact. Here is the opening half:

Born Blind

"Good morning!" came a voice from the darkness which surrounded me.

"This is your big day", A feminine voice followed.

My Heart began to beat harder and harder as I felt a pair of soft hands fumble at the bandages. Round and round went the bandages, would they ever end, I thought to myself. Then suddenly the Nurse's hands stopped. The bandages had gone. I lay still wondering whether to open my eyes after years of darkness. Should I leave the World of darkness which I have lived in for sixteen years of my life. Then as if by reaction my eye lids sprung open. The light was blurred and the faces of the Doctors circled around me. I closed my eyes again. Was I dreaming or was this the real thing. I opened my eyes once more, this time the faces were much clearer. I moved my head from side to side, then I became more daring and I moved my eyes from side to side. Screens surrounded my bed, they were a funny colour, but what colour, the only colour I knew was black. This colour was much brighter, it dazzled me at first but then my sight adjusted to the brightness. I sat up, I look at my hands and my bed, than the Doctor's faces, did I really look like them.

The Nurse held something in front of my face. Immediately it was in line with my head a face appeared in it.

"It's called a mirror, and thats your face." said the Nurse.

I grabbed the mirror and held it closer to my face. The face reflected in it was just as unusual as the screens around my bed. It was something I had never seen before. The Nurse told me to sleep for a while but it was impossible. I was thinking of all the things I would be able to see and do in this new World . . . .

Let us look in detail at the quality of the experience and the way it is being shaped in the longer opening paragraph:

— evoking a mood of expectation ("your big day");
— suggesting the dependence on hearing and touch ("a voice from the darkness," "soft hands fumble");
— indicating the inner apprehension in contrast with the cheerful greeting ("beat harder and harder");
— after the continuing, seemingly interminable "round and round," the decisive moment ("The bandages had gone");
— the attempt to show how, involuntarily, "as if by reaction my eyelids sprung open";
— the expression of partial and indeterminate vision ("blurred, "circled around me");
— a movement from incredulity ("dreaming"?) to greater confidence ("daring");
— the attempt to realise colour for the first time ("brighter," "dazzled").

There is a heightened sensitivity to micro-events and sensations that for a sighted person might count as mundane. Interwoven with this delicate sensory awareness there is a struggle with mixed feelings — expectation, apprehension, almost a wish to put off the experience, and a sense of incredulity when her instincts take over. The writer seems to have caught the uncertainty — even an initial passiveness? — in a girl who is facing a traumatic experience.

Signs of development?

Will the concepts of experience, time, context and integration be useful here, with imaginary stories?

Let us begin by asking what elements of **experience** the two stories are trying to bring together. In "Been Shot in the War" the power of the story lies in suggesting a dazed consciousness, only partially comprehending what has happened; thus external events are disconnected and somehow not under control. Then, in solitude, comes a brief, terrible moment of inner thought, developed symbolically in the sensation of getting colder and colder.

What is embryonic here is explored rather more fully in "Born Blind." This begins with a closed world in which the blind girl lies passive; thus rather than external events it is her **sensations** that are repeatedly evoked, delicately suggesting her heightened awareness that morning. When the central event occurs ("My eyelids sprung open"), again it is sensations that predominate — at this point evoking her confusion in the world that is opening up. As she reacts moment by moment to each sensation, the narration integrates the inner thoughts and the uncertain complex feelings that accompany them. These feelings are dramatised, rather than explicitly commented on (and that's appropriate):

> My Heart began to beat harder and harder . . . .
> I lay still wondering whether to open my eyes . . . .
> Was I dreaming . . . ?
> did I really look like them . . . ?

It is not difficult for the reader to construct felt meanings behind each of these.

What we have just analysed already hints at differences in the degree of delicacy and complexity with which experiences are being shaped.

Now let us turn to the handling of **time**. The first writer has organised a longish period of time into five chunks:

> I was walking just around the camp . . . .
> Next I knew I was on a stretcher . . . .
> So when the Sergeant went . . . I started to think . . . .
> After a while the doctor came . . . .
> Then I went to sleep . . . .

(As it happens there seems to be a missing indicator needed to bridge the move from "stretcher" to "bed"). Each chunk is dealt with extremely briefly. Even the moment that is dwelt on a little leaves a lot to the reader's construction:

> I started to think about my wife and the other soldiers that were not lucky and I was. I felt cold inside as the room getting cold, and colder I thought what would have happened if I was dead.

By contrast the second writer's opening focusses on the events of a few minutes:

> a pair of soft hands fumble . . . .
> the Nurse's hands stopped . . . .
> I lay still . . . .
> my eyelids sprung open . . . .

You feel yourself in touch here with moment by moment experience, and, significantly, that first action is integrated with the sensation and feeling of her heart beating harder and harder. This kind of interweaving continues throughout the first section.

The second writer does mark chunks within her long paragraphs of quasi-continuous action, and these have a very interesting and significant effect, we would say. Thus:

"Good morning!" came a voice . . . .
My Heart began to beat harder . . . .
then suddenly the Nurse's hands stopped . . . .
Then as if by reaction my eyelids sprung open . . . .

It seems to us that these signal and heighten shifts in the dramatic tension. The narrator (and reader) await events with nervous expectation; feel a gathering tension as they are drawn out; register a moment of climax, and respond. The story is taking on the form of a chain of anticipations and outcomes. What is so fascinating is the way this makes room for conflicting and uncertain feelings.

In these respects, the first story is more embryonic. However, at a crucial moment, the writer has found a powerful image, the effects of which resonate through the story. It is an important moment of imaginative penetration.

How about **context?** As it happens, both stories are rather unusual in this respect: one focuses on a man in a state of shock, the other on a girl who has been blind for many years. Other people get a mention but they are not elaborated. So far as setting is concerned there are special reasons, we can see, why this should remain marginal. In seminars with teachers we have wondered more than once whether the fragmentary setting of "Been Shot in the War" arose from a happy accident or from instinctive choice. Who knows? We're content to give the writer the benefit of the doubt.

Penetrating even further into an individual consciousness

The writers we have been studying so far have chosen one specific line of exploration, using imaginary stories to "experience" life through one individual's perceptions, sensations, thoughts, feelings and activities. There are clear gains, as we have seen, when young writers begin to dwell on moment by moment experience. What further imaginative penetration is possible with increasing maturity?

You might like to keep this question in mind, as you read our next example.

Reality

He peered over the landscape of rooftops and chimneys amid the early morning mist and smoke; the common house sparrow chattered on the roof as the first traffic moved in the street below.

He wished that he could be back home, he still called it home even after six months in the city. At this time in the morning he would be eating his porridge, that had been on the peat stove since his father had gone out to milk their few cows. His mother would be rocking gently in her chair, knitting away and every so often dipping into her bag for another colour of wool, regular as the clock that stood on the shelf over the fire. The smell of peat smoke would fill the room and it would be warm, though outside the wind howled and the bay was filled with white horses rushing at the beach and the rocks.

Here in the City the kitchen was a bare white room they shared with the family on the landing below. Here he still got his porridge though it only stood for ten minutes on the gas ring and the oats came out of a packet bought from a shop.

At 8 o'clock he ran down the four flights of stairs, wishing that there were no stairs as there had been at home; and he ran across the road between the cars to catch a bus, a double decker as always. Usually he went upstairs to get a different view of everything, there had only been single decked buses at home and even they only came once in the day.

Today he was going to pretend, pretend that he was home, that the bus was going along narrow roads across the heather or by the sea. It was no use, the people around him were all strangers and outside no hills and sea but tall buildings lining the streets and cars, lorries and buses all determinedly polluting the air. Always noise and only more noise at home there had been noise too, but it was the sound of the sea, the wind and sea birds pestering the fishing boats.

At a quarter to nine he walked into school, only one small boy among so many others. He hated school. At home there had been twenty children in the village school aged between five and fifteen. When winter came and they were snowed up for weeks at a time, only those who lived in the village went to school, and at harvest time no-one at all went as even the Teacher joined in the harvesting. Now he was in a class of forty children all the same age as himself and he had to go to school five days a week, come rain or snow.

When they had first come to the City from the Island he had been excited, he had travelled in a train, he had seen double-decker buses for the first time and they had been held up at traffic lights, and the hotel they had stayed in at the beginning had fulfilled all his ideas of the city.

He remembered, when he was five, his uncle had sent him a book, full of pictures of the City, tall new buildings, flats and houses set in green parkland with trees, and new roads and motorways. He had poured for hours over the book dreaming of living in one of those houses amongst that green parkland, with running water and instant heat and light. Leaving behind the tedious peat cutting, the harvesting and the fetching and carrying of water from the pump.

All his friends had been so envious. They could listen avidly for hours to stories of townlife on the mainland.

"When we get to the City," he had told them. "We're going to have a big house with a garden and trees, just like in those books." Trees were a rarity on the Island, no self-respecting tree could grow in the Winter winds. "There will be running water and electri-c, electric-, light and we won't have a peat fire anymore, you just press a switch and you get a fire, in a box like thing." They all nodded, only a few houses on the Island had electricity. When it became too dark to see, everyone went to bed.

"My Maither tellt me that every house on the mainland has a telephone, are you going to have ane?" Asked Tommy.

"Oh, yes," he agreed mentally added another item to his dream. "And my mother said I'll be going to a school where there are more children than all the people who live on this island." Their eyes opened with astonishment.

I'd be afeared of going to a school with that many childer," to them the Island was their whole world. "Arn't you afeared?" asked his friend Aly.

Yes, he had been afraid when he first entered the school, he felt so insignificant and tiny. All the boys seemed large and horrible, and they had laughed at him with his homespun clothes and his thick dialect. None of them believed that he had lived in a single floored cottage with a well out at the back under the shadow of the hill and no light, such things were unknown to them.

His fantasy had ended abruptly when they first climbed the four flights of narrow stairs up to their new 'home', a two roomed tenement. No garden and trees, no carpet on the floor, a single electric light bulb dimly lighting the gloom and the only running water, was that coming through the roof. The water pipes only went up to the third floor and the only source of heat was the penny slot gas fire.

Now, as he sat in his seat in the classroom, gazing at nothing, he dreamed of a small stone building that was schoolhouse and church with the rows of hard benches and desks and outside the continual roar of the sea and the wind. All this he had left behind for a fantasy of a city but the reality was nothing like his dream.

From the start it is clear that this is going to be a story of moment by moment consciousness. But the present, with its images of "rooftops and chimneys amid the early morning mist and smoke," is almost immediately displaced with the longing to be "back home," and the vivid, nostalgic images that this recalls. When the "bare white room" of the present intrudes itself again, it's the blighted sense of immediate reality which is evoked. What follows is not just a memory but a conscious effort to "pretend that he was home" — to use the imagination to shut out the present with its pollution and machine-made noise.

All this is told not directly in the first person, but by a narrative consciousness which is so empathic with the boy that it can almost look through his eyes and read off, and interpret, what is running through his mind. While some of the language might equally be the boy's ("the smell of peat smoke would fill the room and it would be warm") — marvellously evocative of the mood — much is given a more mature edge and particularity by the narrator.

It's not easy to say at times whether we have the boy's memories or the narrator's articulation of them on his behalf. Is he recalling how "winter came and they were snowed up for weeks at a time," or is this the narrator generalising a description of what may be going through his mind? Up to this point, certainly, his past life *is* being typified, but in the flashback that follows a particular conversation is vividly presented — the actual spoken words of the past break through, as it were, in their direct form, concretely evoking the sources of his self-deception. Through this dramatic dialogue the narrator begins to enforce the contrast between what the boy anticipated and the reality of the city.

Thus in the concluding paragraphs the author offers a more succinct evocation of what the boy might have thought, rather than the fragmentary ideas and images of his stream of consciousness: she is able to interpret and evaluate both the past and the present, probably going one step beyond what the character himself seems to be apprehending:

Yes, he had been afraid . . . .
His fantasy had ended abruptly . . . .
. . . . but the reality was nothing like his dream.

As it happens, then, this story moves in two quite different directions. First, the present life of the boy is interfused with vivid images of the past. If anything he is living more in the past than in the present and this is a very important human possibility to consider. Second, by choosing a narrator who is capable of articulating, synthesising and evaluating, the boy's story is given a distinctive theme. It explores both reality and the way our imagination can be seduced and diverted into fantasy, pretence and self-deception. This is a very profound human concern.

Maturer signs of development

This story acknowledges a new element of **experience.** Life is *not* lived as a continuous present; indeed in our daily lives it would surely be remarkable — even symptomatic? — if memories and scenes from the past did not recurrently erupt into our present "stream of consciousness." Such images and re-enacted moments affect the very flavour and meaning of the present, again and again.

This is especially the case when present reality seems painful, narrow and unfulfilling — as it does to the boy. Memory at first seems to him an escape: if only he could live in the past. But not only does the present keep breaking through; the memories ironically turn round on him and become painful reminders, revealing the naiveté of his past expectations about the city he now lives in.

So just as he now wants to pretend he is "home" in the past, at that time he willingly pretended he was living in the future! In other words the writer begins to understand how both **recollections** and **projections** are intertwined with the present. This is not only a marked shift in the content of inner life; it also gives access to more complex psychological insight.

The past would not be so real to us in this story if the experience wasn't also shaped in delicate and complex ways. It is characteristic of this story that sensations, images and rhythms are used to evoke contrasting moods or states of mind. Thus the writing at times has some of the qualities of lyric poetry — "He peered over the landscape of rooftops and chimneys amid the early morning mist and smoke." In these opening moments the language evokes melancholy and brooding, we feel.

It is interesting to note that these moods often relate to the past (or the present) in general; the memories frequently concern not particular but recurrent events. The images, then, typify the boy's past life, but they are vivid and evocative. And this is appropriate to feelings of nostalgia ("His mother would be rocking gently . . ."). On the other hand, where the past has truths to tell, it is highlighted in a dramatic scene, where the dialogue fully expresses the envy, wish-fulfilment, boasting and self-deception of "his dream."

As regards **time,** the writer is quite original. If she had been dealing with conventional chunks, they might have gone something like this:

- "when he was five"
- on a typical morning on the island "he would be eating his porridge."
- "When they . . . first came to the City"
- Early one morning "He peered over the landscape of rooftops"

It is true that there are chunks — and that they are clearly marked:

— "He peered over the landscape . . . ."
— At 8 o'clock he ran down . . . ."
— "At a quarter to nine he walked . . . ."
— "Now, as he sat in his seat . . . he dreamed . . . ."

These mark off major stages in the morning's events, but "present" time is constantly being dissolved in memories. Something in the "present" triggers the memory by association; early mornings, breakfast, going for a bus, going into school, feelings of fear. So the chronological chunks are less important to the structure than the counterpoint between memories and present events.

In such a story **context** takes on a new meaning. At the baths and the youth club external events were crucial — boys met girls. There was a drama acted out in a setting. In "Reality," however, the drama takes place in inner consciousness. How does this affect our concept of setting, for example? There is indeed a real setting, the city in the present, and it is built up progressively in each chunk, by concrete details. At the same time, within the boy's memories, a contrasting setting is evoked — glimpses of an idyllic past. For much of the time this contrast expresses the boy's shifting psychological states, with an ebb and flow between what he sees, what he remembers, and what he projected.

Thus "setting" becomes a **symbol** for states of being and a vehicle for expressing the boy's psychological turmoil. It is a form of metaphor — an amazing step forward in development.

Perspective and the choice of narrator

Within personal stories there is no choice: you are the narrator. And it is natural, perhaps, that in imaginary stories students often choose to narrate as an "I," as the central character. What this does primarily is to give a privileged access to one character, but not to the rest. When you want to enter sympathetically into the minds of more than one character, however, there is the choice of a "third person" narrator. This is a new dimension to explore in our model of development.

As it happens, "Reality" focuses on a single character and could have been written in the "first person." Yet the author chose a third person narrator. Why did she do so? In the event, the narrator's position is very close to the boy's throughout; she is privy to what he wishes, pretends and remembers. There is even a suggestion at the very start, with the words "he peered," that we may be looking through his eyes. However, she is often subtly able to leave open the question whether she is merely following his consciousness, or has taken on the role of interpreting it. ("All his friends had been so envious . . . . Yes, he had been afraid . . . . All this he had left behind for a fantasy of a city . . . .") This ambiguity leaves room for the narrator to make tacit, or even explicit, appraisals that the character might be only dimly aware of.[5]

This is a reminder that there are at least two major advantages in using a third person narrator:

a) the narrator can both stand back from and move very close to the consciousness and perceptions of one or more characters;

b)   the narrator can also interpret the action and the characters from an independent standpoint, whether sympathetically or critically.

Thus, in this particular example, while the narrator may be following the boy's thoughts and feelings, the language of the story seems, in the main, to be more sophisticated than we would expect from him. We perceive the **presented world,** then, through the filter of the **narrator's consciousness** and forms of language.

Moving into wider social and political experience

One of the primary uses of imagination is to help us look at the world as others see it — to enter into the thoughts, feelings and attitudes of another person. But very few individuals live in total isolation: it is an even bigger step if we can imagine the world not only from one individual's perspective, but also from the perspective of those s/he encounters and relates to. Nor can imagination stop there: this individual and this group are part of a wider society, in which they play varying roles and which shapes their lives.

During adolescence young people will inevitably begin to encounter — and become concerned with — wider social and political experiences. We have already seen how their personal stories can move in that direction. How can imagination extend that range into contemporary experiences that might test or overwhelm them in real life? What kinds of understanding might we hope they will gain?

We want to look briefly here at two pieces which illustrate how much can be gained by 16 or 17 year-olds who attempt this more complex undertaking.

As it happens there is a counterpoint in the strategies the two writers have chosen. The first follows two girls through a day but focuses on the events they become involved in and their joint reactions, rather than on the two as individuals. The second presents an evening's events through the consciousness of a young boy. Thus the opportunities for imaginative penetration and understanding are interestingly different. We begin with the story of the two girls.

Amsterdam Monday

Monday, a very ordinary looking day in the lives of a party of Geography students on their Easter field course. A morning to be spent discussing the planning problems involved in this capital city of Amsterdam, housing, traffic, development and re-building and plans.

If someone had mentioned violence, it would have been relegated to the recesses of all their minds and they would never believe that they might be involved in the very centre of a violent demonstration, that afternoon of a very ordinary Monday.

As they traipsed through the narrow streets to the planning office, the rain poured down their necks and the wind howled down the canals. The office was a building filled with calm and quiet efficiency, even the hustle and bustle of the town outside was muted. The walls were covered with maps, plans, diagrams and aerial photographs of the city. The main topic of discussion was the new Metro. This was to be a semi-underground railway which was to run out to the new suburbs of Amsterdam on re-claimed land, running in a caisson. Plans for this development required part of the old centre of the town to be demolished.

The plans were shown to the party and it was explained to them that the area to be demolished consisted of older houses, some dating back to the 18th C which had been used mainly as cheap accommodation for students and older people. Some of the students felt very sympathetic towards the people who had been evicted, there were some real classic Dutch houses among the area to be demolished.

After a lunch in a small café two girls from the party were seated in the smokey café peering out at the busy world and wondering how to spend a free afternoon in the pouring rain. Shopping was out of the question as all things in Holland were much too expensive, the only solution left, after discarding all museums and art galleries was to explore the town.

A canal bus took them out of the area of hotels, shops and streets lined with cafés, to an older part of the town. All the old, narrow, cobbled streets were quiet and peaceful at this time of day, only an odd cyclist or two passed them. They wandered aimlessly, admiring the old houses and the hidden churches, until they came to a small canal. The only crossing was an old hump-backed footbridge.

Here on the other side, the houses seemed to possess even more charm, tall and gracious with their crow-stepped gables. Then they realised that all these attractive buildings were empty, but the sound of people was much nearer, and the wind howled the louder for the emptiness of the buildings around them.

As they turned the corner, they came upon the edge of a crowd, instantaneously a flash of memory streaked across both their minds — 'the Metro'.

This was the area which was to be demolished to make way for the new Metro. The demolition men were moving in and sounds of the crowd showed what they thought about the men who would pull down these houses.

The two girls joined the crowd as they surged in the street, thinking they would join in a peaceful stand. They soon discovered their mistake, Police were everywhere trying to barricade the area off to prevent further people joining in, while all the crowd were preventing all the demolition men with their cranes and bulldozers from moving in. The policemen each wore helmets with plexi glass shields and they all carried riot shields and truncheons. Standing across all the main bridges looking like Romans with their shields facing outwards, daring the world.

There were students who were obviously squatting in the houses, and the old people who had lived there and the crowd of people who either did not want these houses pulled down or a metro built, a large number of the supporters were tourists or people like the party of Geography students who thought that they would join in. The police were yelling, "Move along, move along now," or rather the Dutch equivalent, the crowd shouted and screamed but no-one moved.

This was a time, the first for many, when it was a battle of them against the police. The police, no longer human but more like identical scurrying beetles with their shields and helmets snarling to the crowd to move away, still no-one moved.

The Police were no longer their friends in this insane stand, all this was new and frightening. Up at the front barriers displaying a jumble of words, all meaningless to the two girls who stood in English silence while around them a chant went up, a catching chant, which soon everyone caught, shouting their loudest, clapping their hands and stamping their feet the mad rhythm filling the air.

Police sirens tore through the streets, and camera spot-lights flashed through the gloomy day. The little beetles with their red angry faces scurried worriedly around the cars, while the banners and placards bobbed and ducked in the wind like sails on an angry sea.

Someone heaved one of the loose cobbles lying in the road at a policeman, the crowd shouted and screamed abusing the police, the city office and the planning office and more cobbles were heaved. Sirens screeched across the canal bridge as more reinforcements for the police moved in, escorting several trucks and a crane but the crowd just became a hysterical mass which doubled as the anger rose among them all, cobbles, bricks and any old muck was thrown at these new beetles.

Suddenly a fierce jet of water was fired at the centre of the crowd by the police with a water cannon, the screams rose and although the two girls could not understand Dutch, the hysterical shouts and screams of the mass could be translated into any language. "Panic!"

An old man, one of the many who had been evicted, was standing on the canal side, his white hair almost the same colour as his papery skin, and as the screams rose in a crescendo, one of the girls noticed with a mental detachment belonging to this insane scene, that he crumpled to the ground like a man who has just been shot, and splash signalled his entering his watery grave.

The girl thought without really registering the fact, "he's probably dead." Her screams rose with the rest as cold water shocked her into reality.

"He is dead, he's dead, he's dead, they killed him, they've killed him," her brain went on saying, like a stuck record. "The police are not our friends, they killed him." Nobody noticed what she was saying, everyone was too busy with their own feelings, she was alone in a mass of people.

The police were using their truncheons freely now as they lashed at anyone who came too close, their identical helmets bobbing up and down from behind their shields.

An empty police car, dented by thrown cobbles and bricks, reared into the air onto its top and with a few well placed matches, the car exploded into light. The hysterical mass danced round it, like witches round their bonfire, or savages round a burning sacrifice to a heathen god.

A swipe of the truncheon hit the girl as she moved and blood stained her fair hair, her companion screamed at the policeman who just ducked behind his shield, expecting a flying cobblestone.

A blue maria, deposited some canisters and some of the crowd were taken up, some struggling, some injured. The canisters were man-handled to groups of policemen who stood in a fence at one end of the mass. The screams of the crowd reached its highest decibel, and a police loudspeaker tried to lecture over the noise, the attempt did not succeed.

Each of the policemen donned a gas mask and the canisters were opened.

The wind blew, — the two girls screamed their hearts out as their eyes stung and wept as though they had got soap in their eyes. Totally blinded by the searing pain and agony and everflowing tears, they blundered back through the crowd. Both with their clothes soaked from the water cannon mounted on the maria like a Gatling gun, one with her fair hair steadily going dark red as the rain and the blood mixed together, the other limped painfully. They reached the back of the mass and ran, heedless of their pain, through the narrow alleyway. Without true sense of direction, only panic and trembling fear of what lay behind them, kept them running through the growing darkness and the falling rain that stung their faces and hands.

Somehow, with luck, they arrived panting, bedraggled, almost unrecognisable and half dead from exhaustion at their hotel. They collapsed, their minds still clouded with terror, their eyes still stinging and their voices hushed from shock.

The next day, the sky cleared and the sun shone, a beautiful Spring day, but it would perhaps never make up for that gloomy Monday in Amsterdam, when the rain poured and the wind howled down the canals and a party of students learned that violence was not just something that appeared on the television newsbeat, but was real and frightening and now formed part of everyday life.

This is another story worth discussing and pondering over in class. In thinking over its achievements, then, let us consider some of the salient things the class might stand to learn.

Two worlds are in contrast: first the "calm and quiet efficiency" of the planning office, its walls "covered with maps, plans, diagrams and aerial photographs . . .;" next "the demolition men moving in," the sounds of the crowd, "the police . . . yelling," panic, and "hysterical shouts and screams . . . ." So the events of the afternoon challenge the calm abstraction of the planners: they have dealt well with the maps and aerial photographs, but have they taken the people into account?

For the two girls (the witnesses) "the old, narrow, cobbled streets" are a refuge, the gabled houses charm them. So we are better able to understand the resistance to their demolition. Indeed, the girls think they can "join in a peaceful stand." The events that follow are what they learn about protest, power and violence.

They see the police: at first "like Romans . . . facing outwards, daring the world;" then "no longer human . . . like identical scurrying beetles . . . snarling to the crowd;" then with "a fierce jet of water . . . fired at the centre of the crowd;" then "using their truncheons . . . lashed at anyone who came too close."

They see the crowd, who "shouted and screamed;" who caught a chant, "shouting their loudest, clapping their hands and stamping their feet" in a mad rhythm. They see someone heave a loose cobble, while others "shouted and screamed abusing the police" and — as sirens screamed — "became a hysterical mass which doubled as the anger rose." They see "cobbles, bricks and any old muck" thrown; a police car, reared onto its top, "explode into light," and "the hysterical mass . . . like witches . . . or savages round a burning sacrifice."

More important, they see the interrelation between the police and the crowd — power and protest, repression and violence. The story has a sharply observed, documentary quality, while at the same time evoking through the girls what it is like to be involved, as innocent victims.

The story presents this experience to us so authentically that after we have recovered from its emotional shock, we can't help asking: What does it all mean? Why does it happen? Can it be prevented?

Our second story follows a similar experience but from a different perspective. Instead of the documentary flatness of the words "Amsterdam Monday," the title of this story has an ambiguous symbolic resonance to it.

The Long Way Home

It was cold, and the gum had lost its taste in Peter Monaghans mouth, and he wedged it precisely into a gap in the empty seat in front. The monster growled underneath, the driver clicked an unseen switch and the exit slammed. Soon they were gliding down Dundonald Road, a car flashed its headlamps and Pete scraped the misty layer from a corner of the window. He knew where he was but thought it better to stay on the bus to the Donegall Road garage. The map was easier to follow that way.

An hour had seen a thorough study of the map and at ten-forty five he stepped off the 'B.32' into a morbid but facinating Belfast. A plastic bag scrunched in the deep overcoat pockets and he looked up at the naked trees and buildings. A broken bottle lay in a broken gutter and the christmas decorations gleamed distantly beyond a camouflaged barricade.

Red, white and blue decorations: where were the green? The christmas trees that lined O'Donnel's first floor opposite Woolworths.

'Business as usual' was the only decoration that hung on Tommy Smiths wooden shop-front — such a change from the glittering display of models last year, and the open street began to fill.

He unwrapped a stick of gum the paper blew to the window with the caged transistors and murky reflections of bystanders. He stared hard again at the record-players, then with the mob at the barricade. A flurry of green and a wailing Land-Rover rammed the vacuum behind the waiting barricade and Pete stood, watched, then ran — ran into the advancing wall several years older, an army of bottles and bricks and militance. Dragged by the screaming, riotous mob, advancing to fire then stumbling, retreating to dodge the bullets, Pete stood — terrified — clinging to a wall with a brick pushed into his hands.

He watched a lad, his own age, collapse to crawl with the white lines and broken glass. He too had a plastic bag, reddened and dripping, as a troop stormed across the street towards him — a mercenary or samaritan? Was it a contorted impression? A physical surge, high and mighty and reaching and smashing and hurting and screaming — why, but why? — but the brick had hit the target.

"You soddin' bastard!" chanted the camouflaged rifle carrier as it swung at face and the December wind blew in his hair.

The decorations shone differently from the back of the police van, the barbed wire and the sand bags of the fortified police station and twenty-foot fence.

Herded, with eight others, into an open hard cell, while a radio sang Christmas carols — peace and goodwill to all men — and "Whats your name sonny?"

The room stank of stale smoke — the repugnence of the uniform with little shiny buttons.

"I said whats your name sonny?"

Another cold hard stare and the boy tried to stop the trickle rolling down his cheek.

"By Christ sonny! I aint got all day! Where do yo' live, how old are yo', where's yo' home?"

A nauseating pause and Pete, for the first time, looked at the officer and it flared up, swiping the boy across the face with its hand. "By God son — you're taking yourself the long way home!"

What are we learning from this story? The opening sets mundane, almost banal events on a bus (wedging your chewing gum "precisely into a gap in the empty seat in front" and scraping "the misty layer") within an ominous context. "A broken bottle" lies "in a broken gutter;" "Christmas decorations" are juxtaposed with "a camouflaged barricade." There are two sides — red, white and blue for one, and a missing green for the other. Tommy Smith's and O'Donnel's — one boarded up, one decorated. Everything has its symbolic significance. Within these menacing streets the boy is then caught up in terrifying physical conflict — "a wailing Land-Rover rammed the vacuum" . . . an "advancing wall" . . . "an army of bottles and bricks and militance" . . . advances, stumbles and retreats "to dodge the bullets." He stands — watches — runs — is dragged — stands again "clinging to a wall" but "with a brick" now "pushed into his hands." Is he a spectator or a participant? The image of "a lad, his own age," collapsing and crawling in the road, and a troop storming across the street towards him suddenly engulf him and he acts blindly, the brick hitting the target — "why, but why?" suggesting the incomprehension he feels. This is hysteria from the inside now.

In the police station the boy is left spent and trapped. His bitter revulsion and silence provoke on the other side first a "cold hard stare," then, as he weeps, an answering violence. The restated question from the policeman reveals the total lack of contact — the blank wall that's between them? "It flared up" depersonalises the antagonist, whose final phrase leaves us wondering who is taking "the long way home." The ending has hardened and placed a political attitude, taking us into a new dimension in the story. Can there ever be peace?

Some implications

Violence is not the only outcome for stories which explore social and political experiences. There are many other settings and outcomes for such stories. The reason why we have chosen these two is that they are outstanding examples of young people trying to understand the violence of our times. Taken together, they also make an important point. In telling such stories, it's possible to simplify the experience so that the effect becomes propaganda. Neither of these writers seems to us to simplify in that way. As we construe them, the attempt is largely or entirely to imagine precisely what happened, while acknowledging complexity or ambiguity in feeling and intention. This is not to say that any writer is ideologically neutral. What we are claiming is that there is a difference, on the one side, between a struggle to get at what experience is really like, and on the other the desire to make a pre-emptive bid to persuade the reader to your position. There is something crucially important going on in writing stories such as the two we have just discussed; it's worth learning and we want to encourage more of it.

How can teachers help?

We cannot expect the average student to find that writing imaginary stories is child's play. As we have said, very few adults do it; why should youngsters be able to? Creating an imaginary story is difficult: when you are telling or writing stories based on personal experience, the central character is well known to you — including his or her inner thoughts! — and so are most of the supporting cast. You have seen the setting, and the plot is ready-made. When you start an imaginary story, you have to create all these.

What do you create from, then? Actually, most of the time, you lean heavily on three sources, at least:

a) elements from your own experience, which you transform and fictionalise;
b) stories you jointly construct in drama, especially when your teachers give you a chance;
c) stories you hear from others, read, watch on television and film, or see on the stage.

As teachers we have to remind ourselves that whereas you are already actively involved in the first two sources, the third source is relatively passive. It's true that in reading or listening to stories you are actively constructing the scene in your imagination; with the rest, however, that is already done for you. So it is likely that the third source — important as it is for most students — will create the greatest dangers for the young writer. The models are powerful, even overwhelming at times; they are difficult to break free from and to use for your own purpose.

We believe this is a great challenge to the English teacher. How can the English classroom become a place where students are at least as deeply involved in fictional stories, poetry and drama as they are in media presentations at home? Once we are on the road to answering that question, we can turn with more confidence to the specific demands facing the student *writer*.

What are these? For convenience, we are going to group four of the most important under the concepts used in our developmental model. Though we shall be dealing with these one at a time, we fully realise that in practice they are inextricable.

What counts as experience?

We have seen from the examples so far how the quality of experience may depend on shrewd observation of external behaviour, on frank acknowledgement of complex inner thoughts and feelings, on an ear for conversation that reveals character, on sensitivity to moods and states of mind, on a delicate awareness of sensations . . . . Even to incorporate and integrate all these elements when dealing with your *own* experience — and to do so with increasing sophistication — seems a long developmental journey. How much more difficult to do this for experiences you are trying to imagine and create. But with help it can be done, even by quite young students. The kinds of help we envisage include the following ways of building an imaginary world:

— Groups in the class take turns to enact an imagined scene, and are helped by the rest of the class to experiment with facial expression, gesture, stance, movement and interaction as they build up an increasingly authentic version of the experience.

— Individuals or groups, working in role, try to present one or other character's stream of consciousness at some key moment in the experience. Tape recorders may be a valuable help here.

— Groups discuss the way different characters might react to an event and improvise a dialogue between them, revealing how each character responds.

— Teacher and students select records of music that might express particular moods or states of mind, and talk or write about what is evoked.

— Students study selected photos with delicate *visual* effects, or *listen* and *touch* things when blindfolded, or are pushed around in a wheelchair . . . in order to help them focus on an appropriate range of sensation in a given scene.

These are some ways of actively building imaginary scenarios. They may be equally applicable when students are *actively* exploring literature, television and film and presenting imaginative scenarios based in these modes of fiction; often enough, parallel work of this kind will itself feed into the student's imaginary stories.

Significant context, of people, setting or era.
When dealing with characters' experiences, you can't help referring to context. What's the background of these people? — where's it all happening? — and when? Whenever students move away from the familiar context (into war, hospital, blindness, a rural island or city centre, another country, an alien situation, historical period . . .) the imaginative leap may make overwhelming demands. So we can encourage them to assemble imaginative resources for the context of their stories in a number of ways:

— The easiest way is to build on a world already portrayed or documented in television and film. This helps them visualise possibilities in the setting, and (given teacher guidance and selection) the life style of a different country or period. There is a problem of course in models that offer a world of clichés and cardboard.

— A second possibility is to build on a literary fiction they are involved in.

— Another method is to fictionalise on your own experience, reversing roles, changing the sexes round, perhaps, but maintaining a world that is already familiar as background.

— For specific, alien contexts — Desert Islands, The Great War, Sailing before the Mast, and so on — students may already be seriously involved and prepared, with help, to root around in the library for visuals, authentic accounts (logs, diaries, ethnographic reports), and other background resources. This is exactly what established authors have to do!

How to deal with time.

The natural tendency to draw on models from war films, television escape series, romantic fiction, science fiction dramas and so on, sets up insuperable problems with time for many students. They have a full-length story in mind, spread over days, months or even years (and inevitably, in the case of books, developed in chapters). Inexperienced writers try to compress all these elements into four or five paragraphs. They need to think seriously about the time-span of typical stories and the amount of "wordage" these commit you to. Among the ways of helping them teachers might consider the following:

— Choosing a genre they are interested in (science fiction, say), students discuss a variety of short episodes that could be written independently — though they might fit quite comfortably into a longer story, later. They might choose a central dialogue, the first impact of an alien place, the making of a crucial decision, reactions to a catastrophic event — anything which gives a first entry into an imaginative world.
— They can read and study short stories, myths, legends and other shorter fictional works (including writing by their peers), discussing how the authors deal with events in time.
— If they feel committed, they can begin to consider longer fictional stories and the use of chapters, studying how other writers (including their peers) chunk time and highlight within a longer time-span.
— When appropriate, they can study and experiment with stories that don't follow the linear time order. Sometimes memories will be interfused with present experience; sometimes there will be flashbacks, or a deliberate decision to start in the middle.

Perspective and choice of narrator

There are a wide range of choices in terms of narrator, and the narrative consciousness that offers perspective on the characters and the events. So far as teachers are concerned, these have been discussed in detail by Wayne Booth. (1961) But we suspect that, so far as most students are concerned, the choice and stance of a narrator is unexplored territory. To make a beginning we suggest at least the following possibilities might be considered:

— Teachers can select interesting examples from more original students and from the books students have chosen for individual reading: the impact and effect of the narrator can then be discussed. (Moffett and McElherny 1966 have a very interesting range of short story examples).
— When reading drafts with individuals or the class, questions of this kind

can then be raised. What differences might a shift in the narrator's consciousness bring about?

— Experiments with "character" narrators and narrators with widely differing viewpoints might be set up, each student in the class choosing a revised narrator for a given episode in a book they have all been reading, perhaps.

CHAPTER 4

Moving Beyond Narrative

Listen again in the staffroom, in the bar, or to children as they meet on Monday mornings. Is it *always* stories that we hear? No.

So: someone does come into the staffroom and starts yet another story about Billy Gristwood, and what he was up to in Geography before morning break. Very soon, though, didn't half a dozen of us join in with:

Yes, that's typical . . . .
He's never remembered his books this term . . . .
Can you do anything with him? I've tried everything . . . .
You know what his trouble is . . . .
The only thing I've found that works with him . . . .
The problem for boys like Billy . . . .
What's our society doing about it, though? . . . .

If we are lucky, and the moment doesn't degenerate into one long moan or diatribe, such a story can become the beginning of a serious conversation.

We move on from narrative, on such occasions, into **typifying**, summing up people's characters, **generalising** from students we know, and **arguing** through social issues as we see them. In the ebb and flow of such conversation, narrative is never far away, either; we are constantly moving back into it, and out again.

How do we know the conversation is serious? People stop to think, they pause for lengthy periods, searching for words. They voice doubts, and offer partial explanations — confessing to ignorance. They may wonder aloud and seem fully prepared to have their opinions altered. Sometimes they may speak steadily, with conviction, opening up a clear perspective on a complicated matter. They may sum up a problem with a natural authority that seems to rise from deeply considered experience. They may argue with themselves, and us — challenging our assumptions as well as their own.

People also listen — and think as they listen, right through the speaker's pauses.

They're assessing those typifications and generalisations, and constructing them in anticipation, sensing out the speaker's line of thought (the experience it's coming from, and where it's heading to). "Go on, elaborate, tell me more," they may respond. Or they may raise questions — genuinely wanting to find out, to test a position, to seek advice . . . .

Conversations of this kind — as we begin to listen to them reflectively — offer the bedrock of experience on which writing beyond narrative can be constructed in the English classroom. Such conversations are never the perquisites of educated groups like teachers. There are four year olds who can talk seriously about life with an adult who wants to listen and respond (Newson and Newson, 1968). So before asking students to write beyond narrative, let's ensure that this kind of conversation is being brought into English classrooms and fostered there. (Britton, 1969, discusses examples first recorded by Margaret Tucker and John Kerry).

Of course, there are no bounds to what human conversation can draw in — scientific knowledge, political and philosophical questions, technological expertise, practical experience, participation in the arts, games and sport . . . . Whereabouts in all this are the special concerns of English? We suggest that they emerge as students begin to look out from a personal centre to the public world, and want to understand its significance for them. Conversely, they are found when students look back at themselves and ask in what ways this public world has been shaping them and their choices in life (taking stock of the outcomes). There are clear continuities, then, with the kinds of experiences being explored in personal and imaginary stories. What changes are the **roles** for the writer and the **ways experiences are shaped and construed;** thus narrative gives way to new forms of discourse, which we will discuss as this section of the book unfolds.

Let us begin with a bridge that seems at times hardly a step away from narrative itself. It marks a first shift of interest, from the drama of particular events to the typical and personal qualities of a character. What opportunities for the writer does this shift set up?

A natural bridge beyond narrative

Considering people in general terms: a younger writer

What happens when a 12 year-old girl, say, starts to reflect on familiar people and tries to convey — even to sum up — the qualities that have become imprinted in her memory and that show what these people mean to her? Our example comes from a young writer who had been struggling for several years with a handicap in reading.

Once again, we suggest you read it aloud.

My Gran and Grandad

My Gran and Grandad are two very smart people. My Gran has grey hair and a soft wrinkled face and has pearl white teeth. My Grandad is small and fat, and is always jolly, and when he is talking he always puts his thumbs in the sleeves of his waistcoat. When we visit them they always remark how I have grown. All evening they will say, "My, how she's grown."

At the dinner table my Grandad is very strict about manners and frowns if anyone picks up a bone to suck. After dinner Gran washes up, and if you offer some help she says, "I'm not helpless," and tells you to sit down and read a paper. When it is time for you to go they say, "Do come again," and they often see us to the station. When the train starts, Gran will wave with a white handkerchief till the train can't be seen any more.

In the summer I go and stay with my Gran and Grandad. Every year my Gran takes out the same old basket so that we can pick blackberries at the rec. While we're picking, Gran always eats more berries than she puts in her basket, so it seems. (Now and then Gran will be missing and when I find her she's picking flowers.)

When she gets back she washes them and boils them to make jam, and she often puts her finger in to taste it and nods her head as if to say, "It's good, even if I do say it myself."

At tea Grandad pastes the jam on his bread — he must like it — and drinks his tea down slowly. After tea they sit down on the sofa, Gran with her knitting, Grandad with his pipe, and an interesting programme on the 'telly.' When it's time to go to bed Gran says, "Nighty night, dearie," and looks over the top of her glasses, and that is all I can tell you about my Gran and Grandad.

Although this affectionate portrait offers typical behaviour ("he always," "they always," "they often"), it is rooted in strong visual memories. Even at the beginning Gran appears with "grey hair," "a soft wrinkled face" and "pearl white teeth," while Grandad "puts his thumbs in the sleeves of his waistcoat." People are evoked in a sharply physical, concrete way. And this is maintained. Thus, though typified, Gran and Grandad are emerging as unique individuals.

What helps the writer, Janet, to keep in close touch with those concrete images? Partly, we believe, the structure she has chosen — probably intuitively. This is a quasi-narrative, first of a regular day visit, and then of regular stays during the summer holidays.

As she recalls her visits, she remembers the rituals of the dinner table, the washing up, and the train leaving. At each point she grasps a significant image:

> Grandad . . . frowns if anyone picks up a bone . . . .
> Gran . . . says "I'm not helpless" . . . . (and) will wave with a white handerchief till the train can't be seen any more.

So here grandparents emerge through significant actions, as time passes during the day. Similarly, in the holidays, we have an outing to pick blackberries, the return to make jam, tea with jam, television and bed. But it is not these summary events that are foregrounded: once again, particular images (remembered with amusement, now?) sum up what these people mean to her:

> Gran takes out the same old basket . . . (and) always eats more berries than she puts in . . . .
> when I find her she's picking flowers . . . .
> she often puts her finger in . . . and nods her head, as if to say . . . .

Grandad pastes the jam on . . . he must like it . . . and drinks his tea down slowly . . . .

Gran says "Nighty night, dearie" and looks over the top of her glasses . . . .

Looking back, then, what is this helping her to do? Although she is typifying people, she does so by catching snapshots of them in action at characteristic moments. As a result, like younger writers of narrative, she can draw on her powerful sense of the visual surface of things. She is able to picture these two people to herself — and thus evoke them for us — with understanding, love and a touch of amusement.

A more mature writer

Signs of further achievement

Our second writer has again chosen to consider someone who is close to her, her brother, who is two or three years younger.

Paul

Paul is sitting in my favourite armchair. I thought how absolutely typical this was of him. He only sat there to annoy me. He did many things which made me angry, but being Paul he always got away with them. I sat watching him. He is only fourteen but could easily be mistaken for sixteen by anyone who does not know him. His face is handsome. His eyes, large and hazel, sparkle with alertness. They are framed with long dark lashes giving them the resemblance of a young calf's eyes. His cute, button nose, covered in freckles, twitches in characteristic fashion. Paul's short brown hair, shaped round his face, enhances his good looks, now, but does nothing for him first thing in the morning. It has a handy way of sticking out at every angle, which makes him look like a scarecrow. He is very fastidious about his hair and will spend a long time in the bathroom trying to flatten it with water. If his hair does not comply with his wishes the world is hit with one of the moodiest people around.

Although only fourteen, Paul is very mature. He has a dark moustache which makes him look very sexy and tough. As this would embarrass him I would never tell him so. He is self conscious of his early development as very few of his friends have fully matured.

As he stands up the full extent of his development is seen. He has the typical male shape already: wide shoulders and narrow waist. His arms are like iron due to the hard muscles which he has built up through weight training. His body is absolutely free of any fatty tissue. He is pure muscle. This can only be from all the sport he does.

His tee-shirt and jeans are particularly characteristic of him. He has a casual attitude to clothes. He does not dress to be fashionable but to be comfortable, unless he is going out.

Although he slouches when he is sitting down Paul walks with the straightness of an athlete. He does not have the annoying habit of putting one hand in his trouser pocket and walking along, as so many men do.

When at home, Paul is a fairly cordial person, but as soon as he meets up with his friends, his personality changes. He becomes lively and full of teenage madness. In the company of our parents, he is evasive and shy about his attitude towards girls. Dad teases him about them which he reacts to with annoyance which is really embarassment. His nose and cheeks turn bright red when he becomes embarassed. It makes him look funny and I cannot help but laugh, which only makes him worse.

Paul came back into the room. He was clutching school books. I looked at him closely. He meticulously set out his pens, pencils and books on the table in front of him. Then he sat, with his head in his hands, just looking at the books. After a few minutes he groaned, he always groaned before starting his homework, and then proceeded to write as quickly as he could: from this I guessed he was doing some French work. This being his least favourite subject he does it as quickly and as untidily as possible. After a few minutes of mad scribbling he put down his pen down and looked at me with his own cheeky grin, which brought dimples to his face. Needless to say, I ended up doing his French as I always do, while Paul sat back and watched television. As to many other things Paul, had taken the easy way out of something he could not do. I know I should not have done the work, but I can rarely refuse him anything; he is far too good at charming people.

Some rather complex things are going on here. Susan has chosen to begin by *observing* her brother, not simply calling up memories. In fact, she does so by what could almost be a conscious device: "I sat watching him." And what seems to have triggered this searching observation is her irritation: "sitting in my favourite armchair . . . how absolutely typical"!

She has every reason to look critically, then, but what comes out to begin with?

His eyes, large and hazel, sparkle with alertness . . . .
long dark lashes . . . the resemblance of a young calf's eyes . . . .
His cute, button nose, covered in freckles, twitches . . . .
short brown hair, shaped round his face . . . .

Despite herself, Susan can't help looking with admiration at this handsome young creature! So these attractive features are carefully selected, and lovingly dwelt on.

A moment later, however, the physical description leads her to touch on some clear signs of his adolescent personality:

If . . . the world is hit with one of the moodiest people around . . .
this would embarrass him . . . He is self conscious of his early development . . .

She is beginning to place Paul in terms of his development, then, physically, socially and emotionally. We have a unique person, but he is also seen in terms of a characteristic phase in human growth.

He has the typical male shape already . . . .
His tee-shirt and jeans are particularly characteristic . . . .

> He walks with the straightness of an athlete . . . .
> lively and full of teenage madness . . . .

She sees his complexity — how "his personality changes," according to the social setting. At home "fairly cordial," but "evasive and shy" about girls; with his friends "lively and full of . . . madness," She can see below the surface behaviour sometimes, too: when his dad teases him, she reads Paul's annoyance as "really embarrassment." And she fully realises that her laughter "only makes him worse."

This middle section is all very general, and deliberately so, we feel. Nevertheless, read very closely, it possibly depends on a tenuous thread of narrative. "I sat watching . . . . As he stands up . . . . Although he slouches when he is sitting, Paul walks . . . . Paul came back into the room . . . ." Agreed, this is a writer who is able to interpolate and sustain long sections of **generalised interpretation** and **commentary.** She can dispense, if she wishes, with the controlling shape of narrative: so when she does choose to use it, at the end, it has a specific purpose. This is a vignette, a specific concrete example which typifies something in Paul's character:

> He meticulously set out his pens, pencils and books . . . .
> Then he sat, with his head in his hands . . . .
> After a few minutes he groaned, he always groaned . . . .
> then proceeded to write as quickly as he could . . . .
> After a few minutes of mad scribbling . . . .

So these are particular actions, read as typical ("always"). But Susan doesn't just leave it there: she interpolates comments that sum up in general terms the significance she sees in this behaviour.

> This being his least favourite subject he does it as quickly and as untidily as possible.
> As to many other things, Paul had taken the easy way out of something he could not do.
> He is far too good at charming people.

What comes out beautifully in this conclusion is both the complexity of her brother and the ambiguities of her relation to this all too charming person.

Looking back at this point, what do Janet and Susan seem to be making of such opportunities to consider people in more general terms? In some ways we feel that what they are doing is typical of the character sketches that emerge in English lessons, but perhaps with more vitality than many. To begin with, as we see, they have chosen people who are close to them and with whom they have important emotional bonds. At the same time, they seem to be learning to be more detached — to recognise foibles in Gran and even slightly wicked manipulations in Paul's behaviour. This mixture of affection and detachment may be an important seed for further understanding.

Trying to sum up someone you know well can lead to significant **generalisations.** You are learning to discern and appreciate typicality — and there are several ways you can do so. You may choose moments in their lives where their actions reveal important underlying patterns of behaviour. You may think of the rituals they follow day by day and what these suggest about their personal style. You may stand back a little further, and recognise how variously they respond to different people, in different social settings.

In terms of discourse, the maturing writer like Susan needs a chance to move beyond narrative. Her discourse has to leave room for — and organise — chunks of physical description, of closely observed activity, of commentary and evaluation of these things, and of generalisations that set the individual character in a wider frame (in this specific case, of adolescent development).

If we compare Janet with Susan we see two significant changes. First, Janet needs to keep the structure simpler and close to narrative, whereas Susan is free to create a flexible and organic form that integrates concrete immediacy and generalised awareness. Second, where Janet is content to present her grandparents' behaviour, leaving its interpretation largely tacit, Susan seeks not only to interpret her brother's behaviour but to organise it within a much broader social framework.

Study of people in a social world

We have started, as we think most students would, with people who are close to them, who they may have known all their lives and lived through many experiences with. Limited character "sketches" of such people offer students who are interested a valuable way of reaching a more summary and general understanding, we would now claim. But they are only one corner of a much wider field.

A new vista opens up when a student has a "serious conversation," with someone, who may be much less well-known, about the social world they are active in and the way they see it. During the last two decades broadcasters like Studs Terkel (1977) and writers like Ronald Blythe (1969) have shown us how much sensitive "interviewing" of this kind can reveal both about the person and about a way of life. Inspired by Terkel's volume "Working," Junior's teacher suggested to his class that they choose someone interesting to interview, discuss the kinds of questions they wanted to ask, and, having taped the interview, produce a written report. Here are some extracts from Junior's final version, which ran to over 1500 words.

> Lois is a state registered nurse and now holds a nursing sister's post .... Lois is twenty-seven years old and is married. She is attractive and friendly ....
> I wanted to know what she really did during working hours in detail. She does her rounds in the morning, reads out reports to nurses (male and female), gives nurses their duties for the day, watches students and pupils use equipment and machines, also makes sure that pupil and student nurses do the right things required. During the afternoons she sets tests (written and practical) for the students and pupils to do and gives them small lectures. After what she told me I said, 'A lot of the students must be frightened of you'. She said she makes them feel comfortable and she lets them feel free to ask questions. She tries not to be a bullish ward sister as she remembers that when she was doing her training she felt nervous at times and did stupid things. I asked if she

ever lost her temper during working hours. She replied 'No'. The only time she lost her temper was when she was a student nurse and a patient threw dirty toilet paper at her . . . .

Sometimes we wonder what makes people choose their jobs. In Lois's case her mother always brought up the subject, as she did nursing. She felt odd when she started her training as she never fancied nursing but eventually she got the hang of it and when she got involved it was too late to opt out . . . . When she gets her holidays (six weeks) she misses the place and always looks forward to getting back on the ward.

That may depress some people, she says, but she has done that sort of work for quite a while and it would take her ages before she could adjust to another job, as she has done this since leaving school. She says many men and women can't stand the sight of hospitals but its different when you actually work in one. People who make these remarks usually go to hospitals to visit someone or have a medical but when you work in one it's just the same friendly atmosphere as a school, office or factory.

Her advice to young men and women is that nursing is a good profession and you don't have to stick to one place or hospital. Nurses are always wanted at hospitals all over the world, and once you're qualified you can earn good money in many other countries. Lois also emphasised that there are many other courses in the nursing field you can do, she says you can always get to the top if you work hard and further your education, as she is hoping to do . . . .

I enjoyed talking to Lois and as you can see she enjoys her job although it was not her choice but she made a go of it and reached somewhere. To end the interview she said she was scared of leaving school to start a life of her own but nursing is her profession now and it would be a waste of time to change it for something else. She can still remember that day, years ago now, when she went onto the hospital ward for the first time, after a six weeks introductory course in nursing school, when she pinned on her cap and the patients called her 'Nurse'.

Clearly Junior is interested in Lois's daily routine: "I wanted to know what she really did . . . ." But this isn't enough for him: he also wants to know how someone with her authority relates to "pupil and student nurses." By challenging her with the idea that "a lot of the students must be frightened of you" he learns how she sees her role — "makes them feel comfortable . . . free to ask questions." In this way, what might have been a rather *impersonal* report of repetitive, clinical activities begins to be *humanised:* we are kept in touch with a person.

It's natural at 17 (Junior's age) to wonder how people got into their work, and what it feels like to work in a rather strange environment. Lois's replies are frank and understanding, while expressing her pleasure and sense of fulfilment in her work. Not surprisingly, she is happy to recommend nursing and explain the opportunities it opens up. But the memory of what it was like to start in her new role brings out a beautifully sharp recollection of the moment when she first "pinned on her cap" and was called "Nurse."

For all Junior's directness — and he did ask some pretty challenging questions — this is a very complex piece of writing. First, although based on a conversation, it is structured as a report, with the questions delicately encapsulated or hinted at:

I wanted to know what she really did . . . .
Sometimes we wonder what makes people choose . . . .
That may depress some people, she says . . . .
Her advice to young men and women . . . .
She said she was scared of leaving school . . . .

This leads us to our second point: here is a new principle of organisation, based on questions, not events. This permits an overview of a person in her social life. It is not an easy task: the form and ordering of such questions — so that they flow on naturally, one from another, — is important both for the conversation and for the report. Junior seems to be breaking into this new form with remarkable confidence.

In part at least, what is encouraging and assisting Junior is the fact that he has interviewed a person, and done so successfully it would seem. He hasn't merely obtained abstracted information without a personal significance (of the kind that pamphlets and documents so often purvey).

So, a third achievement is the balance he maintains between, on the one hand, informing and advising his readers, without at all labouring his role, and, on the other, never losing sight of a person and the way she looks at life — even on occasion catching a characteristic tone in her voice.

This subtle combination of roles for the writer, informing, guiding, advising . . . *and* bringing to life the person who is offering that advice (through the way she perceives her social world) seems to us a central activity in the English classroom.

Implications for teaching

There is a tradition of "character sketches" and "character study" at school that blunts the edge of our perception of people. It treats the writing as a task, aimed at the production of a polished portrait, rather than an opportunity to search your own experience (or someone else's), reflect on it, discover new meanings.

Why write about people (in their social world)? During the secondary years, as students like Janet, Susan and Junior mature, they develop a natural interest in — and, we hope, a deeper understanding of — other people in their lives. Besides, by Junior's age, students begin to imagine themselves in new roles in life outside school, actually to take them on — in weekend jobs, in baby-sitting, in joining clubs, in voluntary social work . . . . The English classroom is a good place to cash in on this natural interest in others, and the desire to extend it.

This implies setting up "classroom conversations" about people whose significance you suddenly notice you are beginning to understand in new ways: friends you may have split up from or who have moved away; people you have become estranged from, who are turning into enemies; people you know well who have hit a bad patch and need help; people who surprise you by taking on a role you hadn't dreamed they could handle; people you begin to admire; people with special expertise or knowledge whom you are coming into contact with and might like to emulate; people whose work or lives capture your imagination . . . .

If an English classroom makes room for such things in conversation, there is more fertile ground for students to *want* to write about people — rather than have a set task imposed on them.

Equally, real conversation about people will soon break through the stereotyped notion that "character sketches" have to take the form of a "descriptive summary." In just three examples, we have tried to indicate the rich potential variety of ways in which we can think about people. Let's summarise here the variety of (tacit) questions that might have prompted these three students:

What usually happens when you go to visit them?
— Can you give us a picture of the kinds of things they do (and say) that strike you as really "them?"
— Are there things about the way they dress, or walk, or look at you . . . that stick in your memory?
What does s/he look like — and how does s/he behave?
— How do you react to them?
— How does s/he react to you — and others?
— And what do these things tell you about them?
Why do you think s/he behaves like this?
— What changes are they going through, do you think?
— How much do you think they understand what they're doing?
What kinds of things does s/he do in his/her day (at work)?
— What does their day feel like: what satisfactions and problems?
— What kind of contact do they have with other people and how does this affect them?
What does s/he have to learn, to do the job well — and to cope?
— What does this demand from them personally, in habits of mind and day-to-day practices?
What advice does s/he have to offer, for someone thinking of taking on the same role?

There must be many more such questions, for teachers to be aware of and, at the right moments, to suggest.

When it comes to writing, a single mould — like "descriptive sketch" — is no help. Some students, like Janet, may welcome or need the support of a quasi-narrative structure, helping them to thread together sharp visual images of typical actions. Others will be ready to look in more general terms, making the break from narrative and organising chunks with varying insights (about different aspects of the person) around a generalised theme or concept. Thus, covertly or not, they may lead themselves to consider wider issues about adolescence, parenthood, old age; friendship and estrangement; or personal roles in work.

When students want to move beyond first-hand experience, to find out things about people they know less well, there's a new demand on them to consider explicitly the questions they want to raise, and thus the experiences and perspectives on them that they want to elicit. This produces a new shaping force for their writing, which can still take a number of different forms (reports, documentary presentations, biographies . . . .)

As people are seen in the context of their working lives, or their social activities, students more and more have to make sense of what we have called "public knowledge" — such as the routines of the ward and the processes of training, in Junior's case. In other cases, the whole of a social lifestyle might have to be understood. The advantage of the English teacher's perspective, however, is that the person always remains important: abstract facts or concepts are given a human frame.

New structures of discourse emerging

If we now look back at the list of tacit questions that seemed to prompt these three students, what does the form of those questions (so far) suggest about discourse beyond narrative?

Suppose we group the questions first: here are two that seem to belong together.

> What usually happens when you go to visit them? — or when he sits down to do his homework?
> What kinds of things does s/he do in a typical day? — or on a typical outing to pick blackberries?

Questions of this kind, when they arise in our "serious conversation," leave us quite close to narrative. We could indeed choose to write a full-blooded narrative chunk about "grandma on the rec;" but we have also the choice of something much more skeletal — the merest outline of Lois's morning. Indeed we could even string two or three characteristic actions on the most tenuous sense of an evening's events — and this *may* be what lies behind our impressions of Paul. What opens the way to a less than fully narrative treatment are certain key words:

> *usually* happens
> *kinds* of things
> a *typical* day

However, the new structural possibilities don't stop there. Let us take a further group of questions (which arise naturally enough from the first group):

> How does s/he behave?
> Why do you think s/he behaves like this?

The first question suggests that we look at relationships between people, either in a frame that is still quasi-narrative, or — if we wish — in a more summary manner. Thus, in Paul's case, his behaviour in the home, with his own friends, and towards girls are considered. This implies a complete break with narrative and a structuring (within this chunk) in terms of categories of setting and the people involved. As it happens, in Paul's case, his characteristic behaviour differs considerably from context to context. This raises the second question, taking us a step further away from narrative structures; thus we are asked for our interpretation of this interesting variety of summary features (or characteristic patterns) of behaviour. We see now that the key words here, if they were made explicit, would be:

> behaves in *general* terms
> in various *types* of situation
> with what possible *general motives* and *causes?*
> with what *underlying values?*

There is a third set of questions — and we are not pretending that is the end:

What does s/he have to learn personally?
What habits of mind or personal qualities does s/he need to develop in order to (do the job well)?
What advice does this lead him/her to offer (about doing the job)?

Questions such as these *could* be answered in narrative perhaps, if we had 50,000-100,000 words available. What is more likely is that they will be answered in summary terms. (Thus, if narrative remains a possibility, it becomes an illustrative anecdote for more general statements.) We are invited instead to consider procedures and processes in abstraction from the specific moments when they occur. We are asked to sum up general "habits of mind," "qualities," "attitudes" and "values." The last four categories indicate how far we now have the opportunity to move into general categories and general statements, in talking about a person.

Standing back from this complex set of structural choices, it is not difficult to understand why an insecure writer might feel safer by staying closer to narrative, while a more sophisticated and confident writer is prepared to be more adventurous, braving demands to weld several different kinds of structuring into a unified whole.

As we have seen, however, when there is a motive to consider and prepare a set of questions, provided these are organised in a related sequence, the student has a natural frame for the ensuing piece of writing — within which the questions may then be retained or left tacit. A frame of questions of this kind can naturally lead to a new form of discourse beyond narrative.

CHAPTER 5

A further natural bridge beyond narrative

Discussing and arguing about behaviour
Let's begin with a flavour of the kind of way people sometimes "discuss and argue" about behaviour. This piece of dialogue comes from Peter, a 14 year-old boy. Notice the *generality* of his title!

On Being a Teenager
"Teenagers, Teenagers," that's what my mum calls us. Sitting in coffee bars, smoking, kicking the ball machines to get extra goes. The juke-box, playing like mad, to the jiving of the teenage beatniks, then soft low music while they kiss and cuddle in low lit corners.

"But not all teenagers are the same mum."

"But look at you, tight jeans, tight jumpers or great big baggy ones, hair right down your neck, and that boy of yours, what's his name? John, that's it, comes up here like a madman on his motorbike, and all he can do is take you to clubs or coffee bars or late night parties. Then you come home hurling down the road, and then both of you go sloppy on the doorstep, it wasn't like this when I was young. You teenagers are all the same."

"No mother, we like to be modern and have fun that's all, but no more than you would if you were young. I like the juke-boxes, and riding on John's bike, and he's a very good driver, and you need tight jeans on the bike so they don't get caught up in the wheels, I like having parties as well and you and dad have a lot of parties too."

"But listen child —"

"Don't child me, I'm eighteen not ten."

"Listen, here comes that mad boyfriend of yours, belting down the road. You'll probably be on the back of it when he has his accident."

"What accident?"

"Oh, you know, all the teenagers have accidents on 'bikes today and he won't get off with it either."

"Oh I'm going out, goodbye."

There are some very important lessons to learn here. In this kind of conversation individual people are assimilated to a generalised category, "teenager." Associated with this word is a whole pattern of anticipated behaviour and attitudes towards it: in fact a stereotype. There are stereotypes about how you look (tight jeans, tight jumpers, hair right down your neck . . .) and how you behave (smoking, kicking the ball machines, kissing and cuddling in low lit corners, like madmen on motorbikes . . . .)

Although we loosely called it a "conversation," what is going on is a head-on argument for much of the time. At one point the teenager makes an attempt to explain and justify her dress and behaviour, but the exchange degenerates — with the introduction of another category, "child"! — and finally breaks down.

Can an English classroom become a place where you can discuss patterns of behaviour and attitudes which you feel strongly about, without ending up in head-on confrontation? Can discussion become a way of clarifying what you think and feel, why you accept some attitudes and reject others? As you get involved in argument about behaviour that is expected of you, can you begin to see your situation within a broader, more general, framework?

Let us keep these criteria in mind as we turn to our next piece, written by Marnie, an inner-city girl aged thirteen.

Why a Girl?

I'm a girl of thirteen going on fourteen. Now that I'm a teenager I'm supposed to buck up my ideas all of a sudden and start acting ladylike. I'm supposed to be sencible and know how to act properly. Well it's just not like that. At the ages of eleven and twelve I was a tomboy. I loved to climb trees, and play football. These are both considered "boyish" things to do. I hardly ever wore a skirt (except for school) and loved to get dirty. The main problem now lies at home. The moment I turned thirteen I kept hearing things like "No! you can't go to the forest to climb trees." and "No! you can't play football, that's a boys' sport." from both my mum and dad. I used to do all of these things before, but now I had to change my whole attitude towards life and act like a girl. The word "act" is the right word, because I wouldn't be doing what I wanted to do, just 'acting' as if I wanted to do it.

Most adults think this way. At the age of thirteen it's about time you started to change. Why change? Why can't you just go on growing up in your own way? I agree you can't go on being a child forever, but I don't think there should be someone pushing you. I suppose they look at acting ladylike an adult thing to do and so they're pushing you into it. Maybe they're just trying to help you come into the adult world, but it would be much better if we were left alone.

With my dad he says one thing one moment and another the next. When I was younger I was allowed to go football with him on a Sunday morning. That was fine, why not let me enjoy myself. Then at thirteen it was "No, not this week. It's not a ladylike thing to do, to go football. Rember you're a young lady now." Who says I'm a young lady? It certainly wasn't me. I just came to accept not being able to go football on Sunday. That was fine, untill I started having friends who were boys. Then my dad would say to me, "You can't have boyfriends yet. You're not old enough." That was the statement of the year. First I'm too old to go football, then I'm too young to have boyfriends. Adults confuse me they do. What is the right age then. It really makes me angry, I don't think they know the "right age" themselves.

When I look at boys, I really think they have the better deal. They don't get none of this kind of trouble, not even from my dad. Sometimes there told to buck up their ideas, but they never get told to stop playing football or to stop climbing trees. That's alright, of course they're boys' sports, and boyish things to do. I have two brothers and my dad doesn't say anything to them he even encourages them. "Why don't you go football this week?" I hear him saying to one of my brothers. Also he said "Haven't you got a girlfriend yet son?" that really makes me mad, my brother's a year younger than I am. How's he going to get a girlfriend if every dad was like my dad.

There is no solution to this problem. Children of my age will just have to go on suffering. Adults seem to have set ideas about teenagers, and once that idea is with them they won't let go of it. When I grow up and maybe have children. I'll try and let them be what they want to be and learn from their mistakes. Knowing my luck though I'll probably get a daughter who will be a proper little lady.

This is an engaging piece to read. It's personal and direct; it's witty and wry; the voices of Mum and Dad have an authentic ring (or moan?); and the sheer thinking is so agile and coherent. If Marnie is as perceptive as this at thirteen, what hopes we can have as English teachers!

What's more, this is a new form of discourse she is learning to organise. Clearly, it arises from speech, from dialogues in her personal life, and that is what gives her voice (and ideas) such confidence and authenticity. We need to pause at this point, then, and examine closely what it is that Marnie is achieving.

Since this is a form of argument, let us start by following through the line of the argument, from paragraph to paragraph. Marnie opens with the current expectations about her personal behaviour that she wants to challenge: "Now that I'm a teenager I'm supposed to buck up my ideas all of a sudden and start acting ladylike." This is her theme, and the first paragraph is rooted in her personal experience, playing on the "sudden" demand to change her "whole attitude towards life" and the irony of "acting" ladylike. In the second paragraph, however, she broadens the argument: "Most adults think this way." And, in asking why, she both makes concessions and counters generalised grounds for their attitudes ("I agree you can't go on being a child forever . . . . Maybe they're just trying to help you, but . . ."). The tone is more dispassionate here, we notice. The third paragraph returns to her own circumstances ("with my dad") and a personal example of his contradictory attitude to what counts as lady-like — "too old to go to football . . . too young to have boyfriends." There is almost a tone of resigned bafflement! "That was the statement of the year . . . . Adults confuse me they do."

Then, in paragraph four, she broadens again to consider the contrast "When I look at boys." Despite her initial generalisation, though, dad can't help breaking in, and then her two brothers ("none of this kind of trouble . . . he even encourages them"). She pounces on a blatant example of self-contradiction in dad's assumptions — and seems to have won her case, so far as the argument is concerned. In the final paragraph, however, she ruefully acknowledges that, when it comes to action, "Children of my age will just have to go on suffering." It is a generalisation again about your status as "child," not "adult." But there is no self-pity about this "suffering": in the end her Cockney wit breaks through!

There is a rich range of achievements here, especially for a thirteen year-old. First there is the coherence of the line of argument, as we have seen. Next there is the flexibility in her perspective: although it is rooted in her personal predicament, Marnie can stand back and see her case as an instance of the general. In doing so she does attempt to acknowledge grounds for the common adult position and to consider that position rationally. Besides, although she feels she is the injured party, her tone never degenerates into the kind of diatribe Peter gave us a glimpse of. The tone is very alive and shifting (exasperated? considered? conciliatory? triumphant? baffled? resigned?) but there is an underlying appeal to reason. It is a serious argument, then, but we are always in felt touch with Marnie's life — with vivid glimpses of her dad. (Perhaps she owes more to him than she realises? — after all, arguing with your dad is a kind of education).

Discussion that draws on wider (public) knowledge

As she tries to challenge new expectations about her behaviour, Marnie finds it sufficient, it seems, to draw on her own experience and that of close friends, making this the basis for her general position. For some challenges, that may be enough; others, however, will require knowledge and understanding that go beyond personal experience and the "everyday" ideas used to organise it. Thus, for example, in our next piece Ann-Marie wants to challenge what we might call "folk-linguistic" attitudes to the way she talks, and in order to do so has to be clearer about "accent," social varieties of language, social attitudes and language functions. Let us see how she copes.

The Way I Talk

I live in London, near Baker Street. "Quite a posh area," you might be saying to yourself, but maybe if you heard my voice you wouldn't think so. I'm not saying I'm a true Cockney born under the sound of Bow Bells, but I do not speak a perfect example of the Queen's English either. The Queen's English, what is it really? Does it mean that we all have to go around talking as if we had a bad cold? I don't hear many people following her example anyway.

You could say I had a slightly Cockney accent, when talking with friends that is. When I'm talking to my friends I can be myself. I don't have to impress anyone like a prospective employer. I interrupt them, we have arguments, but it's me, my real voice. If I suddenly changed to a rather posher accent, my friends would either think I was pretending or that I was 'becoming above myself'.

It's different when I'm with my mum though. When I'm talking to her, I remember not to drop so many h's or use slang as my mum says it sounds terrible. I try to be more respectful in the way I speak to my mum as she's always telling me to speak properly, but what does she mean by this? She comes from Ireland and the way she speaks is far from perfect, but she doesn't understand that my voice is typical of where I live.

Accents and voices of all kinds make up the English language, so who can say one of them is bad? Americans talk how they do because of where they live and so do Irish people and people from Yorkshire, so how can my mum and others be so disapproving of the Cockney accent?

"It's for your own good. Nobody will want to employ you after hearing your voice." This statement is one I hear almost every day from my mum. But why should the way I speak matter? It doesn't mean that I'm any less intelligent than a person who speaks 'properly'. A person reading the news for example, would still be reading the same news whether she was speaking with a posh accent or a Cockney one.

When talking to teachers or adults other than my parents, my speech changes for the third time. Instead of my usual chatty self, I speak awkwardly and am very conscious of what I say and the way I say it. I used to muddle sentences and forget what I was going to say but as I get older I'm gradually overcoming this handicap.

I think it all started when I was younger, as I used to have a speech impediment. Nothing I ever said sounded right so instead I decided not to speak much at all. I became very shy and withdrawn and because I didn't mix much with other children because of the impediment, I became very lonely. Nobody can fully understand a situation like this unless they've gone through it themselves. I was teased by a certain group of ignorant juniors and so I got this idea into my head that I was different, unlike other children. The only time I ever felt at ease was at bed-time when I used to imagine that I could turn the light out and become invisible. This affected most of my younger life but I'm happy to say that my speech has improved greatly since then. It has taught me two very important lessons though. Firstly, that nobody is perfect, but more importantly that it doesn't matter how a person speaks, or how they dress or walk, it's the person itself that matters.

People are judged by their voices which, as I have experienced, is wrong. Some people are under the impression that it's a status thing. If you're poor you'll have a very Cockney, common accent and if you're rich you'll speak very genteelly and politely. But does this mean that all Cockneys are rowdy, rude, ill-mannered thugs and rich people are sweetness itself?

Everybody has a different voice and different way of speaking. The way you speak is as natural as the way you walk or eat and nobody has the right to criticise it. I don't think I should have to change the way I talk to pass a job interview as, unless I was going to be a speech therapist, it would be irrelevant to my job. I speak English which is a language. Language is a means of talking, communicating, being understood. People do understand me so why should it matter?

If we all spoke the same, life would be very boring. We would lose our personalities and if this happened, we would lose our individuality. Nobody has the right to comment on the way a person talks as their speech reveals their character and if you take away a person's character you're left with nothing but skin and bones.

It's a very serious, thoughtful discussion. There is a neat analysis (and understanding) of the way Ann-Marie's own speech varies in three different situations — with friends, with mum, with teachers. She has become consciously aware of variation in her own spoken "style" (as it is called) and that already offers a richer conceptual frame. Besides, there is also an attempt to set a wider perspective, as we shall see.

Again, we want to trace the line of the argument. From the start there is a playful reminder about people's social expectations: Baker Street implies "quite a posh area" — and what, by the way, does the Queen's English imply? So her theme is established as social attitudes to "a slightly Cockney accent." Three of the paragraphs that follow show how pressures from different social groups affect both her accent and her articulacy. Talking with her friends, she doesn't "have to impress;" with her mum "she's always telling me to speak properly;" talking to teachers or adults "I speak awkwardly and am very conscious of what I say and the way I say it." Already, however, interpolated into these general observations on her own speech behaviour, there is a refutation of her mother's attitude by appealing to a wider perspective on major regional or national accents (Irish, American, Yorkshire . . . alongside Cockney).

The reference to her awkward self consciousness with teachers leads to a fragment of personal history which certainly explains past difficulties, though at first glance it might seem a diversion from her main theme. However, from the "ignorant" teasing, she learned "two very important lessons:" first, "nobody is perfect," and, second, "it doesn't matter how a person speaks," it's the person that matters. This links back to her theme and forward to the three generalising paragraphs with which she concludes.

> People are judged by their voices which . . . is wrong . . . .
> The way you speak is as natural as the way you walk . . . [and "irrelevant" so long as people understand you.]
> If we all spoke the same . . . we would lose our personalities . . . .

These propositions advance the argument into the public domain: she is making judgements about widespread social attitudes in the light of general principles.

Once again, we find an impressive coherence here. In this case there is a valuable movement from a clear analysis of her own speech behaviour to a principled statement about social attitudes to speech. This seems to us to be buttressed by rather more sophisticated understanding and knowledge of the way we use language than everyday conversation offers. The discussion is not couched in technical terms, but her concepts are clear.

Finally, there is an interesting difference between Marnie and Ann-Marie. Whereas Marnie was centrally concerned to argue *against* her dad, as it were, Ann-Marie wants to articulate the principles and practical understanding on which she bases her own attitudes. It is significant that her argument with her mum is only incidental.

Discussing behaviour more impersonally
Both Marnie and Ann-Marie can argue confidently and frankly about their own behaviour. Sometimes, this isn't possible, though. Students may feel they do not know the teacher and their classmates well enough to discuss personal issues with such openness. The culture of the home may also run against such open discussion

of personal matters, and this has to be respected. In addition, there may be issues that raise painful feelings and which students prefer to distance by discussing in general rather than personal terms.

When you want to keep yourself out of the discussion, you have to take an impersonal stance (and fictionalise any personal references, if you choose to make them). Fortunately, this impersonal stance may have some advantages in other respects: it may help you to focus on the level of general ideas, beliefs and attitudes. Besides, thinking about a wider canvas (even if you have your own problems in mind) can be a help.

It is with these thoughts in mind that we include in this chapter Narinder's views on "the problems affecting Asian youngsters in Britain." At the time she wrote this, Narinder (age 16) was betrothed to an Asian boy she had not yet met and the marriage was due to take place the following year. Like several other similarly betrothed girls in the class, she was worried, so her teacher decided to organise a series of lessons exploring Asian culture. This is the context in which Narinder wrote.

My views on the problems affecting Asian youngsters in Britain

Asian youngsters face many problems in today's society. The most difficult of these problems to solve are the ones that take place at home. The atmosphere in an asian home is very tense, and communication between the parents and the children is almost none existing. These problems are present because the parents were brought up in such a different society than today's youngsters and also because of culture, the need for maintaining this important element at home is very great. It is this lack of communication at home that causes all the problems outside the home, the young asians become shy and find it hard to make friends and to actually talk to people of their own age and to older generations. The parents also produce a barrier between themselves and their children, this barrier is mainly made up of a lack of trust. Although the parents may consent to their children, for example, continuing their education at college as in the Sixth Form, the youngsters can be sure that in the back of their minds the parents will doubt their decision and a lack of trust will be present. It is this that makes the asian youngsters feel unwanted and, even, degraded, but what they must realize is that the parents believe that they are doing the right thing by bringing their children up with no exposed emotions, and by restricting their activities.

Asian youngsters are so much protected by their parents and by the community that they will, in most cases, give up any ideas or hopes for future careers and will just want to settle down and live in a less restricted and peaceful atmosphere. Respect and reputation play a very big part of family life in an asian community, and to maintain these elements the youngsters are protected to a great extent. This protection restricts asian youngsters from being anything but asian. This protection or restriction was mainly formed when the first asian people came over to England to live and work, they brought with them their sons and daughters, most of whom were newly weds. The elders of the time saw that if these newly weds were not restricted and made to stay asian, and keep the culture, they would get out of hand and be lost to the western way of living. It is in this kind of atmosphere that our parents lived in and they have continued to use today's youngsters as they were used.

Asian marriages have also started to cause many problems. Most youngsters will go through with an arranged marriage because they believe that they have no other future and that this way they obtain the best of both worlds, the eastern and western way of living. These marriages are very destructive, future careers are ruined because the question of marriage is mentioned when the youngsters are going through many mental and physical problems. Most young asians will go through with an arranged marriage because they would feel rejected in any other society and because they believe that their own kind would turn against them. These marriages particularly put pressures on asian girls. Young asian girls find it very hard and difficult to talk and communicate with their parents, this means that subjects, such as careers and further education, are undiscussable with parents, and so the girls suffer a great deal mentally and also withdraw into themselves.

As far as the future generations are concerned, I feel that it will take a long time for them to escape the asian system and the problem it causes. Although, we, the future parents, will show our emotions more openly towards our children and help them with our experiences, the elders and the asian society in general will, I feel, take over when the children come to the age of adolescents. This, I think, will form a barrier between us, the parents, and the children of the future.

In the circumstances we read this as a fairly heroic attempt to talk rationally and calmly about a situation that for Narinder herself was deeply disturbing. There are repeated struggles to understand and articulate the attitudes of the parents, the elders, and of the generation who "first . . . came over to England to live and work." We feel there is a discernible effort to present their perspectives and the values they want to preserve. What makes this hard is her strong sense of the problems created for the younger generation, like herself. She does not hold these back — indeed, she may sometimes overstate or over-generalise. There are some particularly painful moments, though: "so the girls suffer a great deal mentally and also withdraw into themselves." But a kind of courage emerges at the end; here, as her own voice breaks through, she faces with a kind of stoical calm the possibility she can foresee: "This, I think, will form a barrier between us, the parents, and the children of the future."

Looking at the line of argument both within the paragraph and beyond, we see recurrent signs of struggle. Home is "tense;" communication between parents "almost none existing." But she tries to look beyond the individuals to the cultural forces behind them — "the need for maintaining this important element." Almost immediately, however, she reverts to the consequences: the youngsters' shyness, "a lack of trust," and the parents' self-doubt in decisions that cut across cultural norms (about "education at college," for instance). As she acknowledges that girls like herself may feel "unwanted and, even, degraded," she tries to wrench herself back to seeing the parents' position and "what (the youngsters) must realise."

In the second paragraph, there is a sustained effort to offer a rational justification

— partly in historical terms — for the parents' wish to "protect" their children, to see them "settle down . . . in . . . a peaceful atmosphere," and to gain "respect and reputation . . . in an Asian community."

Set alongside this is the elders' fear that the youngsters "would get out of hand and be lost to the western way of living." But again, in the paragraph that follows, her own preoccupations and conflicts burst through. Her statements basically present a depressing state of affairs — the line of argument is broken.

> They believe that they have no other future . . . .
> These marriages are very destructive . . . .
> they would feel rejected in any other society . . . .
> the girls suffer a great deal mentally . . . .

If the argument has indeed broken down here, it is almost certainly because of the pressure of personal feelings. But the writer rallies, in the last paragraph, as we have seen, to reach a personal, coherent but bleak conclusion.

The achievements here are of a different kind from those in our two previous examples. Narinder's problems (insofar as they are typical) won't be resolved in argument with mums and dads, and the thinking expressed in this piece helps her to understand why. Behind her parents' attitudes she is trying to realise the determining forces of a community (on whom those parents depend for "respect and reputation"). She is placing her own tensions and those of her group, within an overall conflict between "Asian" and "Western" values. She is not so much "arguing" as attempting to explain to herself and others how such a conflict comes into existence.

There is little or no comfort for her here. All she seems to have gained is a recognition that there are more than personal forces at work: she is just part of a wider struggle by a minority culture to preserve its community values while accommodating to an alien society. Fundamentally she is looking to the teacher as an understanding adult: it is not judgements on her "composition" that are needed here.

Implications for teaching

Written discussion and argument, as they have been traditionally taught, have all too frequently turned into sham exercises — or completely outfaced the student with their demands for sophisticated public knowledge (Dixon and Stratta 1982, 1983, 1986). Yet these three examples begin to show the opportunities that are there, waiting to be tapped.

During the secondary years most of us wake up to the fact that, as one of our students said: "You don't have to look far for where I got these opinions — they're the same as my father's!" What is more, given the opportunity to reflect on the forces that have shaped their lives, students begin to recognise that their gender roles, social class, ethnic group, religion and political affiliation . . . are things they have been born into, and often have accepted unquestioningly. Because this is a period of trying to find out who you are and where you stand in your particular society, however, it is natural for many students to discuss and argue about these things. It is not surprising then that Marnie is arguing about what being a girl (or a boy) should mean, that Ann-Marie is questioning social (or class) attitudes to her regional accent, or that Narinder is struggling, caught in a clash of cultures. The idea that it is necessary to invent a special breed of "argumentative" topics, or drill in the techniques of argumentative "debate," *manifestly misses the point.*

Once again, an English classroom has to be a place where fundamental questions about how you behave and the attitudes and beliefs that underpin your behaviour can be aired, explored and challenged. Going back to Peter's cameo of family argument, we are warned that, for argument to be fruitful, people have to learn to listen, to recognise and respect serious attempts to think through a personal issue, and to have strategies in discussion that go beyond rejecting ideas and opinions out of hand. So there are important roles for the teacher here both in setting up a climate where civilised discussion can take place and in setting an example as a thoughtfully responsive and understanding listener.

There is a lot to learn. To begin with, as you look at the family and social forces that are shaping your experience and values, you inevitably begin to generalise from your own life. This has its dangers: your personal experience is limited, and your perspective is bound to simplify its complexities. For both these reasons it is important to listen attentively to other people. Almost inevitably, if you take account of the serious implications of what they say, your generalisations will be qualified, developed — and enriched. Sometimes, too, the other "voices" will come from outside the classroom, to enlarge the "public" knowledge available in a discussion: we will see more of this in our final chapter.

Secondly, you learn by differing. By attending carefully to the behaviour, attitudes and opinions you disagree over, you begin to analyse and evaluate the grounds for your initial position. You have to learn to weigh up the rational basis for your generalisations — to confirm, modify or even abandon them. This is the benefit you stand to get from dialectical exchange, especially if someone in the teacher's role can help you to reflect on the whole process.

In all this you have to learn a new subtlety in your use of (and attention to) language — especially the language of generalisations and general categories.

Further structures of discourse

We want to distinguish here two broad, and no doubt overlapping, motives for written discussion and argument. On the one hand, there are conflicts over how we should behave (and the attitudes and beliefs that support this); on the other, there are curiosities about the significance of a given line of action (and the underlying attitudes and beliefs). Conflicts lead us to argue, though this may be tempered into discussion; curiosities lead us to discuss, and perhaps to reflect and analyse in a more ruminative way. The difference affects the way stretches of discourse are structured.

As it happens, conflict is the motivating energy behind all three of our examples. Marnie has to start acting lady-like — to "change my whole attitude towards life." Ann-Marie doesn't think she "should have to change the way (she) talks." In Narinder's case, symptomatically perhaps, the conflict is much more submerged but "this protection restricts Asian youngsters" and "it will take a long time for them to escape . . . ."

Let us see how this affects the discourse. Marnie — like many younger writers — keeps us concretely in touch with the spoken arguments behind her writing:

> No, not this week. It's not a ladylike thing to do . . . .
> You can't have boyfriends yet . . . .
> Haven't you got a girlfriend yet, son . . . ?

Elsewhere there are fairly obvious indirect quotations: "I'm supposed to buck up my ideas . . . and start acting ladylike." The predominant structure of whole sections (almost all the opening paragraph, for instance), is a kind of re-enactment of argumentative exchanges at home.

There are other structures, however. In Marnie's second paragraph, for example, having generalised about what "most adults think," she challenges their attitudes:

> Why change?
> Why can't you just go on growing up in your own way?

This has a very significant effect on the structures that follow; the conflict is tempered and there are the signs of a real discussion:

> I agree you can't go on being a child for ever, but I don't think there should be someone pushing . . . .
> I suppose they look at acting ladylike . . . .
> Maybe they're just trying to help . . . but it would be much better if . . . .

There is a kind of negotiation going on — and the thinking is in some respects richer for it.

With Ann-Marie, her mother's attitude is explicitly incorporated (and countered) but it is hardly central. On the other hand more generalised positions are certainly questioned and challenged at times:

> The Queen's English, what is it really . . . ?
> So who can say one of them is bad . . . ?
> People do understand me, so why should it matter . . . ?

Some of these are almost addressed to the readers, to challenge their beliefs or provoke further thought. Ann-Marie realises that she has a very widespread social attitude to take on, as she addresses the core position (not the person), working directly at the level of ideas, rather than through a form of dramatic dialogue. If one of the high peaks of Marnie's method comes as she pounces on her dad's illogical advice to her brother, the parallel in Ann-Marie comes as she attempts a proof:

> I speak English which is a language.
> Language is a means of talking, communicating, being understood.
> People do understand me, so why . . . ?

Encapsulated within structures of these two kinds, both writers begin to raise questions about their opponents' use of language:

> The word "act" is the right word . . . .
> These are both considered "boyish" . . . .
> The Queen's English, what is it really . . . ?
> but what does she mean by this . . . ?
> a person who speaks 'properly' . . . .

They are not taking for granted the tacit assumptions lying behind these words; this is an important sign of their maturation and makes complex demands on structuring.

Besides the analysis of categories hidden in the language there is also, at times, encapsulated analysis of a social state of affairs. Thus, using herself as an example, Ann-Marie takes time to show how speech varies in different situations: "when talking with friends . . . when I'm talking to [my mum] . . . when talking to teachers . . . ." These statements about her behaviour help to show that "accent" is a complex form of behaviour. This brings us to Narinder.

Fundamentally, Narinder's piece is about conflict but, for personal or cultural reasons perhaps, she chooses not to challenge anyone directly. It may be too painful. There are certainly moments where a kind of exchange emerges:

> Although the parents may consent . . . the youngsters can be sure . . . parents
> will doubt their decision . . . .
> It is this that makes the Asian youngsters feel . . .
> but what they must realise is . . .

In a sense, the last clause is an attempt to "answer" the challenge from the youngsters (like herself?) who feel "degraded."

The paragraph that follows might have continued that answer about "what they must realise" — and it partly does. There is a half-explicit argument that "restriction" is a form of "protection" — "this protection or restriction," she says. The attitudes of the parents and the community *are* represented; their hopes that the youngsters "will . . . want to settle down and live in . . . a peaceful atmosphere," winning "respect and reputation," "[keeping] the culture," rather than "get out of hand and be lost to the western way . . . ." But there is no question of winning over herself or her readers by this careful analysis of their position. It is merely presented to us in a distanced way — and, incidentally, shot through with half-submerged reservations (*so much* protected . . .*give up* any ideas or *hopes* . . . *just* want to settle down . . .) Significantly, the internal conflict is left unresolved at the end. It is a reminder that in considering structures of *discourse* we must never lose sight of structures of *feeling*.

CHAPTER 6

Looking further afield — new roles

When the conversation is about grandmas and younger brothers, or where you stand about your dad's attitudes to boy-friends and your mum's to your accent, *you* are still at the centre. But when it turns to special social experiences you have had, bringing you into contact with opinions, attitudes and forces further afield, there is often a significant change in what is discussed. New kinds of questions are raised. How should somebody else set about doing these things? What attitudes have other people encountered? What makes some people act as they do? What do people beyond ourselves (and like us) need to hold on to? You are invited to take more than a personal perspective on your social experience, to draw lessons from it, to reflect on it — and possibly to propose a line of action.

When questions like these are raised in an English class, the students they are addressed to have to take on new roles, which demand new levels of social maturity. This is not easy — after all, how egocentric our lives are much of the time! These roles not only imply a maturer perspective; they also call for more knowledge, more careful investigation, more social understanding, a more complex analysis than we normally get by with in day-to-day life.

Questions like these can lead in many directions. The best we can do in this chapter is to explore a few of these, suggesting the kinds of roles student writers can take on — and the wider range of readers they can begin to address — as they learn to reflect on their social experience and to take such questions with increasing seriousness.

Offering advice: an elementary example

Some of our younger students wake up with surprise to find that a small step they have taken into the social world counts for something in other people's eyes. They are suddenly thought of as experts, perhaps, who can be turned to for advice — in general terms. It is assumed, that is to say, that their experience is typical and that the perspective they can offer on it must be valuable. It is very gratifying to be taken seriously: when they are asked to put their advice down more permanently, in writing, even the less confident writers can rise to the occasion.

In the example that follows, Simon has organised his "Guide to a paper round" into a booklet divided into sections. Here are the first three:

How to apply

I would find a good repatuble [reputable] firm. You walk in and ask for a vacancey. If there is one they will ask you your age. You must be 13 yrs or older. They will ask you your address and other details. Also ask what you will get paid. If the wage is below £3.50 I would turn down the job. They will probably ask for you to come in the next day.

Here are some repatuble [reputable] shops.

1. Dillons
2. Stars
3. Evening mail agents
4. Birmingham Post agents
5. N S S

Your first round

An important part of having a paper round is getting to know your boss or bosses. Walk in — with an happy attiude [attitude] and say "Good morning". This will show your boss that you can socailize with people. The head boss (mainly male) nine out of ten times will come with you on your first round. A round card may be provided. This would be a typical example:

Ethel st		112	sun
1	mail	Avary Rd	
4	sun	2	sun
12	times		
Grant st			
55	times		
	F T		
69	tele		
100	mirror		

This also may apply to an evening round. A map may also be given. [For] example:

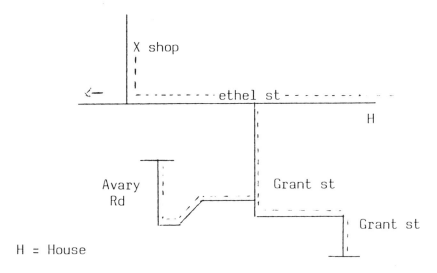

H = House

Start your round with confidence and don't get worried if you make a mistake. Another piece of advice is use a bike.

Mistakes

When you make a mistake do not PANIC. You will offacasly [obviously] make a mistake on your first round, Either

1   Go back to the shop
2   Phone shop when you get back home
3   Don't tell anybody

There is a delightful confidence in the opening tone: "I would find a good repatuble firm." Here is somebody we can trust! More good solid advice follows: "If the wage is below £3.50 I would turn down the job." There is some shrewd psychology here too. It is not only sensible to "walk in with an happy attiude;" it also "shows you can socialize." "Start your round with confidence," he tells us and equipped with his sample round card and map we can well believe we might. Then comes the reassurance about the mistakes we "will [obviously] make on our first round." Hm . . . which of the three lines of action shall we take, though?

If we look at the achievements of this young writer, within his simple style they are really quite complex. First, he has given himself a sense of control over the wide range of advice he could offer by designing a series of sections, each answering a tacit question.

How do you apply?
How do you make a start?
What kinds of problem are you likely to meet?

It's a sensible order.

Second, within the section he has a good sense of priorities, bringing up early the question of age, for example, and neatly postponing the list of reputable shops to the end of the section.

Finally, he is reassuringly concrete with his map and typical round card, but reassurance doesn't stop there. It's quite thoughtful of him to realise that the inexperienced boy or girl going into a shop might need encouragement to be cheerful, and not to panic if they make a mistake.

Implications for teaching

For students like Simon the confidence to write like this most often comes from interested discussion and questions. This gives them a chance to discover and rehearse what they know and an incentive to put it down in writing. Then as they set about organising their advice into a piece of discursive prose, they can use a set of questions as their guidelines — some of these questions may actually have been asked, others may be imaginary. Once collected, they have only to be organised into a sensible order and they will provide a valuable supporting structure. This is where our help as teachers may be needed.

Once the booklet is written, our next job is to find readers for it — to "publish" it. But there are possibilities for further learning. Take the section on "Mistakes." If we read this back to a class, it should not be difficult to stimulate a discussion about how you should behave. We think that Simon has something to learn here and might be interested to listen to the discussion and summarise his impressions of it.

As students mature, there are further possibilities within such a task, and beyond it. How about the boss and your relations with him or her? What kinds of social know-how does the job call for? What kinds of attitudes do you meet from the clients? What counts as a reputable firm? Questions of this kind can be explored from the perspective of many other jobs besides paper rounds, and many other forms of social encounter.

In general, then, we are suggesting that an important role for the teacher is to lay the ground for qualitative shifts in students' understanding of their social encounters — to encourage groups of them (and a class in conversation) to dwell on the more penetrating questions that arise, and tactfully to prompt these when the opportunity comes — in discussions, or in reading back sections of their writing.

Taking an investigation deeper

When you have taken an active part in social life — like Simon — you have "experience" to offer, and probing questions will often make you turn back and have a sharper look at what was going on. So you stand to learn something fresh, because you are asked to take a serious role — to reflect, inform and advise.

What other ways are there of penetrating into social experience? We have already seen Junior interviewing a person whose work he wants to know more about. And there are other ways: a further choice is to go and observe, or better still to act as a participant-observer. These are ways of entering into social experiences about which you are deeply concerned but largely ignorant.

Teachers who are interested in social enquiry of this kind have hit upon many imaginative, enabling strategies. For instance, our next students, Penny and

Susanne, took part in a sustained investigation into provision for handicapped people in their area of Birmingham. This included being pushed round for a morning in a wheel chair to find out what a physically handicapped life was like.

Here are some extracts from what they wrote as a result of that experience.

"Never were there so few facilities for so many, so needy as in Kings Heath!"

"No, sorry luv — I've not got time to stop and get 'er on 'ere"

"Can I help?"

"A wheelchair won't get in here"

"Can I help?"

"Out of the question — It will block up the gangways"

"Can I help?"

The above are reactions from the general public of Kings Heath Birmingham, to people who are handicapped in such a way that they are confined to a wheelchair. The above are verbal reactions, the visible ones again vary from a pleasant smile to the embarrased person who so obviously looks away, to the members of the public who stare, to those who simply "carry on".

However, people's reactions are not the only problem the handicapped person faces as they come into Kings Heath. It is hard for the active person to understand just how difficult a wheelchair is to manover (manoeuvre) on the narrow pavements, and just how limited provisions are, and to feel what it is like in a wheelchair — some people have to face that every day of their lives . . . .

* * * *

The provisions for the disabled in Kings Heath.

Recent research into the provisions made for the disabled in Kings Heath has revealed a serious neglect of these members of the community. Admittedly, they are a minority group in society but, they pay their rates like everyone else and should be considered accordingly.

The 1961 Provisions of the Disabled Act places a moral obligation on the Council to consider the disabled as a part of society but it appears that Birmingham City Council need more than a moral obligation and a genuine concern for these people before actually taking notice.

Having spent an afternoon in a wheelchair in Kings Heath I was appalled at the facilities; or rather the lack of them, and in some cases the totally ignorant people who treated me as some type of freak . . . .

Conversely one man helped me up the kerb in the wheelchair and was openly friendly and kind. It just seems a pity that we cannot all follow his example without being patronising or over-sympathetic.

When examining the facilities in Kings Heath and referring to the 1969 Act it is blatantly clear that not only the Council disregard the handicapped but also shopkeepers.

Under the Act the disabled have rights of access to all public buildings but unless you are as 'light as a feather' literally, the steps up to the library are virtually impossible to mount in a wheelchair. If by some remote chance the impossible is achieved and access has been realised, the narrow corridors or passages within the library are not only a nuisance to the person in the wheelchair but also a nuisance to the general public.

The public toilets it seems, are not required by the disabled as yet again there is no provision for accessibility and steps lead down into the toilets.

Pavements are a nightmare for the person in a wheelchair and anyone pushing it. Uneven, badly laid slabs present a problem and the kerbs are really very dangerous.

Very few kerbs have a ramp or slope on where you want them — in Kings Heath where the majority cross at the end of a road, and if you are lucky enough to actually cross on one it is probable that there is not another slope directly opposite. This means a hazardous detour — dangerous to the disabled and the public in general. To be fair the new Pelican crossings do have ramps but no improvements have been made to existing crossings . . . .

* * * * *

It is interesting to recognise here how much choice students have in drawing together what they have discovered and in presenting it to readers. Penny launches into a dramatic impression of people's reactions, counterpointing the negatives with the refrain "Can I help?" Is there already an appeal — a plea, even — to the reader? Shrewdly, too, she notes that the visible reactions are as varied and important as the verbal. Susanne, on the other hand, sets her investigation in the broader canvas of her local community's moral and legal responsibilities. Her ironic tone challenges the reader, and the Council. You feel the sharpness of her perception and indignation. "The public toilets it seems, are not required by the disabled . . . ." Help isn't enough, she reminds us, if we cannot offer it "without being patronising or over-sympathetic." Both these students have learnt something that they are deeply concerned to communicate.

We have chosen these extracts to illustrate a variety of achievements. Penny has found a succinct way of presenting the social world of the handicapped. It is concrete, dramatic yet summary. Because it has form, there are powerful implications lying behind her snatch of dramatic dialogue. And the list of visual reactions fills out the character of the social exchange you can expect. She recognises how difficult it is "to *feel* what it is like" and, very effectively, has begun to help us readers to do so. Susanne has a different purpose (and readership) in mind: her writing is more of a political rebuke.

> serious neglect . . . they pay their rates like everyone else . . .
> places a moral obligation on the Council . . . blatantly
> clear that not only the Council disregard . . . there is no provision . . . .

It is not a diatribe, but a considered and withering attack. The impersonal stance of "Recent research . . . has revealed" probably adds a touch of authority to her personal reactions ("I was appalled"). The range of hazards she covers — public buildings, the library, the public toilets, the pavements (and, later, shops) — reinforces the sense of a systematic investigation. Each is documented.

Clearly, then, both these sixteen year-olds are learning to address an adult readership and to be taken seriously by them.

Implications for teaching

Social investigations of this kind open up many fields that may lie beyond students' direct experience, but frequently enlist their interest and concern. Beyond the physically handicapped, a class might consider social responses in their communities to groups who are socially deprived, to ethnic or religious minorities, to the young and the old . . . .

As we have seen, the scope and form of the investigation needs a good deal of thought. Can the students enter into the experience as well as observing it? Where will participant-observation be appropriate, where simulation (as here)? What range of settings, problems or issues will need to be taken into account? When will public knowledge — like the provisions of the Disabled Act, or the decisions of a local Council — need to be introduced and studied? Preliminary answers to such questions have to be thought through beforehand and possibly discussed in detail with the class, so that they can actively participate in creating a structure for the investigation.

Where students are venturing well beyond the boundaries of their social experience and confidence, there is also a need to alert, sensitize and forearm them in serious preliminary discussions based on interviews and role play, for example, and perhaps to give them personal support in the early stages.

As students become committed to such an investigation and feel they are learning a good deal, the question arises: who do they want to report to or tell about their findings? Is it other students in the school? — is it parents? — is it local community workers, representatives, or councillors? — is it a government office? There may well be a range of possible readers. Having decided who to address, the next question is how best to select from their particular experiences (in the wheelchair, in this case), and their general understanding. As they experiment with ways of organising what they have discovered, there is the question of finding the appropriate stance and tone.

So finally the test of such reports lies in their effects on real readers outside the class. Thus the teacher needs to make opportunities for this to take place, and for considered feedback from readers to writers.

Responding to social pressure

Social encounters aren't always things we plan. Sometimes they happen to us — in our school, in our club, in our street, in our neighbourhood . . . . We face the consequences of other people's attitudes and actions, and sometimes we want to resist, probe or endorse them. When these actions lie in the public domain, likely as not, public letters, circulars or notices may be called for.

Our next writer, Michelle, faced one such encounter, felt she wanted to respond, and turned to her English teacher for help. She decided to write a letter to the local press. This took a lot of effort, but after several drafts it was sent off and published under the title "Books Open Doors."

> Editor, The News: Recently two women have been coming into the J...H... Junior High School Library and checking out books overnight. It's not that we're upset about their checking them out, it's that they

refuse to speak to us. We were informed by a concerned teacher that they were compiling a "report" on certain books. Yet, being they won't speak to us, we have no idea of exactly what kind of report.

Our only idea (being that books are being permanently removed) is that they are looking for so-called "bad books." I read a lot and have never read a book that has any reason for removal. Some books deal with sex, divorce or suicide, which are parts of life that we must deal with.

Think for a minute of the real world. How can we really know what's beyond our front door if it's slammed back in our faces? Books help us open that door and realize what's out there, so we are aware of the different situations and people we will encounter. There are deaths, kidnappings and murders out there.

Books that explain these problems don't make us have these problems. Instead it makes us appreciate our awareness.

Some people who have problems suddenly pop into their faces might commit suicide or even turn to drugs to cope with everyday living. Many skilled writers such as Susie Hinton ("The Outsiders," "Tex," "Rumblefish") and the anonymous author of "Go Ask Alice" know a side of life we haven't seen yet.

So, in conclusion, these women of the "censorship committee" should pause and think for a minute of the lives you could save if you didn't remove that book — even the lives of your own children.

This is quite an accomplished letter. The opening suggests something clandestine is going on from which students feel shut out, but the tone, if slightly aggrieved, remains measured: "it's not that we're upset . . . it's that they refuse to speak to us." Raising the possibility that "bad books" are to be removed, Michelle questions this category and the attitudes lying behind it. As her argument against its tacit assumptions develops, she appeals first to her own experience ("I read a lot and have never . . .") and then, more powerfully, begins to generalise. "Think for a minute of the real world." Her image of the door "slammed back in our faces" is a strong expression of the affront that she feels is being offered to students in her school, but it is also valuable in making her case that books "help us open that door . . . (and) appreciate our awareness." Moving from the defence to the attack she imagines, in general terms, "people who have problems suddenly pop into their faces," whose ignorance of life may be a fatal handicap. This leads her, in conclusion, to make a powerful appeal to "these women of the 'censorship committee'" to "pause and think for a minute."

It's part of the strength of the letter that it invites a reasoned response in which she, and her peers, are taken seriously, even if the reader disagrees at some points.

Implications for teaching

What a difference here from the standard text-book lesson on letter writing or argument. This fourteen year old has something important to say and has found an appropriate form. The letter is alive.

Nevertheless, we must recognise how much learning may lie behind such letters. Fourteen year-olds may often have to be reminded that, however deeply they care about an issue, blasting off in public about it may be counter-productive. They have to take seriously the attitudes and opinions of other people as well as their own. So in such cases as this, they must ask themselves precisely what attitudes and assumptions they have to counter. And they must learn, possibly from others in their class, which of their own attitudes and assumptions won't stand up. Once again serious conversation (and analysis) offers the essential basis for such writing.

When it comes to the writing, it's important to recognise when to be tentative (about the possible motives of the two women, for instance), where personal experience is appropriate, where concessions may be needed, and where to assert your general beliefs strongly and firmly.

Michelle's letter is a reminder of many occasions when what is done to teenagers, or proposed on their behalf, is open to question; and equally of other occasions when, in the students' view, the interests of others is being attacked and ought to be publicly defended. With many of our newspapers, too, it would certainly do no harm if such serious and considered letters were regularly coming from schools!

Making a cultural statement
Michelle's letter is a defensive reaction to a social encounter. In this section we want to move to a more positive role. Sometimes students feel they have gained such enlightenment from their own cultural and social experiences, that they have a real desire to put their ideas forward, knowing they are worthy of consideration and respect from a wider audience. Here is Bolal's response to an invitation to convey what she gained from music, drawn from a published collection of Black writing.

Reggae Music is a Source of Strength Because . . . .

Reggae music is a source of strength because it is an invisible link between all Blacks. Music is one thing that all Blacks have in common from the beat of tribal drums and high-life music deep in Africa, to the Calypso, Reggae and latin music of the West Indies and parts of South America.

Far from the Motherland this music is one of the few things that Blacks, both old and young, hold on to. It is a strong element that we can easily identify with. We can communicate with each other. While concentrating, but still relaxed, we cruise along on the rhythm and the beat; drinking in the notes like a sweet, soft drink, soaking in the beat like rays from the sun.

Out on the streets of the strange, cold land of Britain, Africans scorn West Indians and West Indians scorn Africans. Why? There are many reasons, but once they are all in the same room listening to reggae music, they begin to feel closer, more understanding and tolerant. They look around feeling proud. Why? They have discovered their brothers and sisters. As the warm vibes reach into their flesh, their bones, their minds, they relax, they forget their scorn. (Peace).

Some Reggae music puts forward great messages which make the people realise things they had overlooked. This is a further strengthening of the bond of brotherhood. (Realisation).

Sometimes the music is not warm or strong enough to reach into the dark inner parts of some people, hardened over years of degradation, humility in bondage, brutality and injustice. These people may refuse to be touched in their long struggle to become accepted and be like their

European counterpart. The way then to express this wish is to refuse to have anything to do with Black roots, from which reggae music stems. They scorn Black Music, clothes, wording, poetry and attitudes, but once this thick coating of ice is melted the true person is found. This can be done the easy way by persuasion and realisation of one's true identity, or by the hard way; total isolation from the Black society and cold rebuffs from the white society. After this process the person may be found ready to join in the loud colourful gaiety which the music exudes. Ready to be wrapped in the rainbow waves of the music, they are ready to relax and be themselves.

Standing in a crowd of people at a Reggae concert, there is a feeling of closeness, warmth and security. Being there with the music and the brothers, every person is just as important as the next. Strangers greet each other with familiarity and proud smiles. They hold other strangers hands as they sing and rock to the music. They know where they are now. They know who they are and they have found their long-lost brother or sister, and they pick up from where they left off years and years ago.

When a teenager approaches his or her parents asking or telling them that they are going to a party, the parents seem reluctant to let them go. Sometimes they don't. Sometimes they do, saying they can't understand why a person should want to stand up all night listening to the deafening notes blaring from home-made boxes but as you say your good-byes, can you detect a distant look in their eyes? A look that says, "yes, I know too well — you've found something that will show you, teach you, explain to you some things in life". They know only too well the feeling of closeness, brotherhood and identity.

Without any form of Black music, our people would surely feel more isolated and there would be more hostility amongst each other. It would be like being suspended in a vacuum without strong emotions but by adding the music and stirring gently, we live more freely. Reggae music is one of the hopes for Black unity.

Given that this article is couched in such general terms, what surprises and delights us is the poetic quality of the language which catches us into its shifting moods and carries us along — especially if we read it aloud. "We cruise along on the rhythm and the beat; drinking in the notes like a sweet, soft drink, soaking in the beat . . . ;" words like these express the rhapsodic intoxication of the music. On the other hand, "Out on the streets of the strange, cold land . . . ," with its ominous ring, sets up the conflict which immediately follows. There is a real attempt to contemplate and understand the struggling humanity of those people who don't want to be touched: "the dark, inner parts of some people, hardened over years of degradation, humility in bondage, brutality and injustice." But the piece doesn't remain solely at this generalised level — there is a shift as if into a real concert, with glimpses of strangers greeting each other "with familiarity and proud smiles." And later of a parent's look that says, "Yes, I know too well."

What more can we say about the impressive achievements of this 16 year-old? What makes the piece more than a paean of celebration of her Black identity is the recurrent acknowledgement of the conflicts to be overcome, in a hostile land, between Black and Black; conflicts within Black people who "refuse to have anything to do with [their] Black roots" but still meet "cold rebuffs from the white society;" conflicts in parents who seem reluctant to acknowledge the crying need for this symbol of Black strength, yet "know only too well" the desire for closeness, brotherhood and identity." Each time, she imagines the music dissolving their conflict "as the warm vibes reach into their flesh, their bones, their minds . . . ." As in music, there is a sense of poetic structure; from conflict to resolution, conflict to resolution . . . .

At the same time this is a political statement about one thing that "all Blacks have in common," and about "the hopes for Black unity." She too wants to put forward a message, to "make the people realise things they had overlooked." Through Reggae they find "their long-lost brother or sister" and "they know where they are."

Further Structures of Discourse
In the last two chapters we have moved into the domain of what is conventionally known as Argument and Exposition (or Informative writing). In our view, these terms conceal more than they reveal. In particular they have been used to set up expectations of rigid models of written discourse, which are found only in classrooms, never in real life. When we recall the uses of serious conversation in our own lives, it seems necessary to recognise two broad dimensions:

— the range of overlapping purposes that conversation incorporates;
— the range of levels of abstraction: that is to say the movement between narrative and generalisation, and between higher and lower levels of generalisation.

Reviewing the pieces in the last two chapters, in order to discern underlying purposes, the reader will see that each falls into sections, or chunks, which:

advise, inform, explain, illustrate, warn . . . . (Simon)
dramatically present, analyse range and variety, inform . . . . (Penny)
(and) report, argue a case, analyse and evaluate . . . . (Susanne)
report, surmise, refute, ask for consideration (of a proposition), challenge assumptions, appeal for second thoughts . . . . (Michelle)
state general beliefs (or personal truths), express states of mind, explain, offer resolutions . . . . (Bolal)

There are more refined ways of expressing these purposes, but it is clear enough that many pieces of writing will serve to integrate a group of purposes, rather than follow through a single purpose. In part, it is the multiplicity of purpose that often makes the writing of prose so complex in its demands on young writers, for each "purpose" arises from a tacit question, and the difficulty is how to put these questions together in an integrated string.

The form of each question turns out to be vital, and that brings us to our second dimension, the levels of abstraction. Sometimes the questions may be construed in terms of an individual person. Thus, Simon answers "How to apply" in terms of "you" walking in. He treats his particular experience as typical. So what he says remains quite concrete. At other times, however, the questions may be construed in terms of whole groups, like "people who are handicapped" or "all Blacks." So the circumstances are thought about and interpreted in much more general ways: "Far from the Motherland this music is one of the few things that Blacks, both old and young, hold on to." Pretty clearly, Bolal is drawing on personal experience, but she chooses to generalise from it and the thinking is in more abstract terms. Answering the question in terms of a "typical" individual or a whole set of people makes quite a difference, then.

In a similar way, sometimes the argumentative exchange is, tacitly at least, with an individual person. "You can't have boy friends yet. You're not old enough," says Marnie's dad. "She is always telling me to speak properly," says Ann-Marie of her mother. However, it is equally possible to construe the exchange in terms of generally held beliefs, attitudes or ideas. Thus Ann-Marie recognises that "People are judged by their voices" — it is a social propensity she has to deal with, not an individual quirk. General attitudes of this kind have to be countered at a more abstract level, by drawing on general principles and critical knowledge. "Language is a means of talking, communicating, being understood . . . . Everybody has a different voice and a different way of speaking." She is beginning to move into the level of ideas and theory. And the basis for this lies in her developing ability to analyse and categorise her own behaviour (treating it as typical).

What strikes us, looking back over the more mature writers in the last two chapters, is their remarkable ability to move flexibly from one purpose to another, and to move back and forward with ease from concrete particularities to abstract ideas.

Envoi

This book is about the writing of prose — and by no means all the prose that we would hope to find in an English classroom. There is a complementary book to be produced about writing that arises from reading literature and studying the media.

And prose itself isn't the only form English teachers want to foster: there are poetic and dramatic forms, too. These two offer powerful ways of presenting and reflecting on experience, both personal and social. Let us close, then, with a poem, written by Jane, a 12 year-old, in response to Richard Church's poem, "The Pigeon."

World made of concrete

Concrete buildings, concrete roads, concrete pavements,
People's hearts are getting to be as hard as concrete,
Even little children's minds are turning to concrete,
For the birds and the animals, they can turn their
Backs on this world of steel girders and concrete houses,
But, for us, we don't seem to realise how free and much
More above us are the cats of the wild and fowl of the
Air, just for being simple and happier minded,
How they can ignore us and our concrete hearts and ways,
And run free.
But, we just don't realise that we are becoming imprisoned
In a world of concrete, even the animals, free as they are now,

Are being imprisoned by us, in our concrete homes,
for *their* home was long ago, ours also,
But man is eating up with his concrete buildings,
And yet, some day, a dove will fly down from the
Heavens, and pick at the thin thread,
That keeps our buildings and concrete homes erect,
And down they will all tumble, like a babies' bricks
Chock-a-block, all the iron, girders, and concrete,
Fall onto the silly little concrete people,
Murdered, by what they themselves have made.

REFERENCES

Douglas and Dorothy Barnes, "Cherishing Private Souls," in **Timely Voices,** ed. Roslyn Arnold (Melbourne: OUP, 1983), 35-52.

Ronald Blythe, **Akenfield.** London: Allen Lane, 1969.

Wayne C. Booth, **The Rhetoric of Fiction.** Chicago: University of Chicago Press, 1961.

James N. Britton, **Language, the Learner and the School.** London: Penguin, 1969.

Department of Education and Science, **Aspects of Secondary Education.** London: HMSO, 1979.

J. Dixon and L. Stratta, "Argument and the Teaching of Writing," in **The Writing of Writing,** ed. Andrew M. Wilkinson (Milton Keynes: Open University Press, 1986).

J. Dixon and L. Stratta, "Argument: What Does it Mean to Teachers of English?" **English in Education** 16, 1 (1982), 41-55.

J. Dixon and L. Stratta. **Character Studies — Changing the Question.** Southampton: Southern Regional Examination Board, 1985.

J. Dixon and L. Stratta. **Teaching and Assessing Argument.** Southampton: Southern Regional Examinations Board, 1982.

J. Dixon and L. Stratta. **Writing as a Participant Observer.** Southampton: Southern Regional Examinations Board, 1984.

John Foggin, "Writing for an Audience" in **Case Studies in English,** ed. Patrick Scott (London: Longman, 1983), 21-31.

Peter Medway, "What Gets Written About?" in **The Writing of Writing,** ed. Andrew M. Wilkinson (Milton Keynes: Open University Press, 1986).

James Moffett and K. McElheny, **Points of View.** New York: Signet, 1966.

John and Elizabeth Newson, **Four Years Old in an Urban Community.** London: Allen and Unwin, 1968.

Horst Ruthrof, **The Reader's Construction of Narrative.** London: Routledge and Kegan Paul, 1981.

Studs Terkel, **Working.** London: Penguin, 1977.

STUDENTS' WRITING

The Outcast	JMB/TWYLREB exemplar folders; J. Dixon and L. Stratta "Achievements in Writing at 16+," booklet 1 Schools Council 1981. ERIC ED 208 389.
My First Date	Ibid.
When we first went down	John Foggin and his students at Boston Spa School; J. Dixon and L. Stratta, "Writing as a participant-observer," SREB 1984. ERIC ED 220 829.
The Volunteer	Paul Norgate and his students at Waseley Hills School, West Midlands; J. Dixon and L. Stratta "A range of informative writing," SREB 1982. ERIC.
Day 1: Monday 19 Oct.	Eric King and his students at Peers School, Oxford; J. Dixon and L. Stratta "Writing as a participant-observer," SREB 1984. ERIC ED 246 424
Been Shot in the War	J. Dixon and L. Stratta, "Achievements in Writing at 16+," booklet 2. Schools Council 1982. ERIC ED 216 366
Born Blind	Ibid.
Reality	Ibid (JMB/TWYLREB exemplar folders).
Amsterdam Monday	JMB/TWYLREB exemplar folders; Dixon & Stratta "Achievements in Writing at 16+," booklet 1 Schools Council 1981
The Long Way home	J. Dixon and L. Stratta, "Evaluating imaginary stories," SREB 1982.
My Gran and Grandad	Geoff Heywood and Janet, Walworth School, London Paul J. Dixon and L. Stratta "Criteria for writing in English" SREB 1981. ERIC.
Lois is a state registered nurse	Sue Crump and Junior from Northumberland Park School, London; J. Dixon **Education 16-19: the role of English and Communication.** Macmillan, 1979.
On being a Teenager	Peter, Walworth School Magazine
Why a girl?	Margaret Atkin and Marnie at Haggerston School, London
The way I talk	Ann-Marie Twomey in "Say What You Think." Inner London Teachers' Centre, 1986.
The problems affecting Asian youngsters	Pauline Cowan-Monaghan and Narinder from Holt Comprehensive School, Birmingham
Guide to a paper round	Brian Hirst and Simon at John Flamsteed School, Derby
Never were so few, & Provisions for the disabled	Joan Markham and her students at Swanshurst School, Birmingham
Books open doors	Marsha Looysen and Michelle at Junior High School, Minot, North Dakota
Reggae Music is a source of strength	Bolal Lamal and the 1982 Prize-winning anthology, *Afro-Caribbean Education Resources,* Inner London
World made of concrete	Bernard Newson and Jane, at that time at Crown Woods School, London

based on a true story

Silver Mane
The Tale of a Wild Horse

Written and Illustrated by
Mary Miller-Jordan

Silver Mane ~ The Tale of a Wild Horse
Text Copyright© 2012 by Mary Miller-Jordan
Illustrations Copyright© 2012 by Mary Miller-Jordan
ISBN 978-1475074581

For more information please visit
www.highcottonhorsefarm.com